Creative Tensions

Creative Tensions

*Civility, Empathy, and the Future
of Liberal Education*

BRIAN ROSENBERG

PUBLISHED BY
MACALESTER COLLEGE

Published by Macalester College
1600 Grand Avenue
St. Paul, MN 55105-1899
macalester.edu

Illustrations in this book by Julie Delton.
Book design by Brian Donahue / bedesign, inc.

ISBN 978-0-9905744-0-8
Printed in the United States of America.

Dedication

To Carol,
Adam,
and Sam,
in gratitude
for their love
and patience.

Acknowledgements

The list of people to whom I owe the privilege of working
at Macalester, and from whose work, dedication, and
generosity I benefit, would be too long to include in an
acknowledgments page. I will limit myself here, therefore,
to recognizing those whose help was instrumental to the
completion of this little volume: Tommy Bonner,
Kate Abbott, David Warch, Rebecca DeJarlais Ortiz, and
especially Lynette Lamb from the Macalester Advance-
ment and Communications offices, and Brian Donahue,
who designed the book layout. Their work has been
outstanding. Any errors or infelicities in the text must
be laid at my feet.

Contents

Introduction

Seeing What I Say

In *Aspects of the Novel*, an elegant and influential work of literary criticism, E. M. Forster cites a surely apocryphal anecdote in which some befuddled soul exclaims, "Good gracious! . . . How can I tell what I think till I see what I say?" This is more or less how I have felt while reading through the various essays and speeches that I have fashioned during my decade as president of Macalester College. The recurrent themes, the enduring influences, the annoying habits: all are much more apparent to me now that I have taken the time actually to see what I have said. Reading oneself is not always pleasant, but it is instructive.

Profoundly clear is the fact that my tenure as a student and teacher of literature—about a quarter century, from my college years through the conclusion of my time as an English professor—is the chief influence both on my style of writing and, more important, on the values that form the basis of my work as a college president. A good many of the novelists and poets that matter to me are present in my ramblings: Dickens of course, but also Keats and Blake, T.S. Eliot and Matthew Arnold, Twain and Flaubert and Mary Shelley—along, to be honest, with a little Seinfeld and Mary Tyler Moore. What I have chosen to take away from their work, and what informs on a daily basis my own, is the understanding that without kindness toward and connection to others, we are liable to be both unhappy and creators of unhappiness. An education that does not reinforce this message is fatally incomplete. This may seem hopelessly naïve to those who believe that the value of a college should be measured wholly in vocational and economic terms, but (as Dostoevsky has shown) there is something to be said for radical innocence.

I have also been influenced by great educators and writers about education: William Bowen, former president of both Princeton and the Andrew Mellon Foundation, who has done as much as anyone in our time to help us understand both the strengths and the inequities in our colleges and universities; Stephen Carter, Professor of Law at Yale and author of *On Civility*; Eugene Lang, creator of both the "I Have a Dream" program and Project Pericles. They, too, understand that education is a complex business with multiple objectives but always, at its center, the preeminent goal of shaping both individuals and societies that are more wise, just, and humane.

The themes to which I return again and again in my writings and remarks are similar enough to suggest either that I am hopelessly stubborn or, more charitably, steadfast in my beliefs. Of course I emphasize in whatever form I can what the late Richard Warch, president of Lawrence University for 25 years, liked to call the "value and virtues" of a liberal arts education. Anyone in my business who is not convinced that such an education provides unique and lasting benefits both to the individuals who receive it and to the society that supports it should be in another line of work. One of the central jobs of the president of a liberal arts college is to capture that conviction in words of clarity and passion, even at the risk of redundancy. I reserve judgment on the question of whether I have managed to be either clear or passionate, but I can say with confidence that I have mastered the art of being redundant.

What I had perhaps not fully realized before rereading these pieces was the extent to which two features of a liberal arts education have come to dominate my sense of its peculiar importance. The first of these I refer to in various contexts as "empathy" or, citing Keats, "negative capability": it is, put simply, the ability to step away from one's own history and biases, at least for a moment, and see the world through the eyes of another whose history and biases are quite different. I believe that this ability, along with the willingness to exercise it, is the essence of humanity in its highest form and also what is sorely lacking in so much of our public policy and public discourse. A liberal arts education should, through exposing one to various cultures and disciplines, various histories and faiths, various ways of understanding and processing information, make one more empathetic. If it does not, it will have failed in perhaps its central purpose.

The act of reading a poem or working in a laboratory should not just make one smarter, though surely it does that. It should serve as a reminder that Plato was right: what each individual takes to be reality is in fact a small portion of a much larger whole that is infinitely more complex and meaningful. A liberal arts education is not about getting to the truth, but about discovering that the quest for truth has no ending.

The second feature, which is intertwined with the first, is civility. By this I mean not merely politeness, but the ability and willingness to listen with care and respect to the appropriately expressed opinions of those with whom one disagrees and to express one's own opinions with similar care and respect. Without civility there can be no fully functional learning community; without civility, as Stephen Carter has argued, there can be no fully functional democracy. I will leave it to others to judge whether what we are experiencing today in our great democratic experiment are the consequences of a breakdown in civility and whether the new forms of communications enabled by digital technology have encouraged that breakdown. (Actually that is disingenuous: my own answers to those questions are an emphatic "yes" and "yes"). Regardless of how one thinks about these complex issues, I believe that a sound liberal arts education should serve as an antidote to and a defense against the uncivil. In this one regard, at least, it should remain defiantly old-fashioned.

Even a casual reader of my writings will note that while, I hope, I am never less than civil, I do manifest from time to time some annoyance, generally in the form of sharply worded irony. This is especially true when I am addressing public policy or public utterances having to do with higher education. Most college and university presidents steer clear of this stuff, probably for good reason. I am constitutionally unable to do so. While I do not consider myself an especially political person, I do plead guilty to a low level of tolerance for poor reasoning, arguments unfounded on evidence, and demagoguery. When I observe these things—and the past few years have provided ample opportunity for such observation—I become something of a mongoose in the presence of a cobra. All I can say to those who wish that I would be more restrained is that for every piece of this kind that I do write, there are ten more than I have composed in my mind and tossed into a mental shredder. There are only so many battles one can fight.

In writing and speaking about Macalester in particular, I have been inclined to emphasize the aspects of the college that are most distinctive: the urban location, the global focus, and above all else the fierce commitment to the idea of education as a path to responsible citizenship and to service in communities large and small. This is not meant to diminish the importance of the foundation of excellence in the disciplines of the liberal arts upon which everything at the college is built, but to suggest that Macalester is possibly a better place and is surely a more interesting place because it takes seriously the relationship between what one knows and how one lives, in the deepest sense, a useful life.

Unique is among the most misused and overused words in the English language, but it may indeed be the case that Macalester is unique among American institutions of higher education in its longstanding combination of signature features. I am tempted to observe that we are unique as well in our tendency to argue among ourselves about pretty much everything, but in truth that tendency seems to be widespread, if not universal, among the colleges and universities with which I am familiar. While this can be frustrating and even counterproductive when decisions need to be made and changes embraced, it is a perhaps inescapable corollary of the independence of thought rightly championed in all of our mission statements. Colleges and universities may simply be the institutional equivalent of the great, sprawling novels of the 19th century: what Henry James famously described as "loose, baggy monsters," filled with memorable characters and multiple plots and glorious excesses of style, but without the sort of precise organization and deftness of execution that James (like some members of Boards of Trustees) favored. Perhaps, as some modernists believed, the baggy monster is hopelessly outmoded. Or perhaps *War and Peace* and *David Copperfield* and the American residential college will continue to stand the test of time pretty well.

While I am not nearly as old as was William Butler Yeats when he published his great, elegiac poem "The Circus Animals' Desertion," I have thought often about the opening of that poem as I have reflected upon what to say about my decade at Macalester.

> *I sought a theme and sought for it in vain,*
> *I sought it daily for six weeks or so.*
> *Maybe at last, being but a broken man,*
> *I must be satisfied with my heart...*

I am *not* broken, though my back is not what it once was and my rotator cuff has seen much better days. And I hope that it will be a long time before I can say "at last" about either myself or my time in St. Paul. But I am drawn very powerfully to the notion that in the end the most difficult yet most important subject about which to write is one's own heart. And so here is what is unexpressed in my public utterances, but what is in my heart: what a strange and unexpected thing it is that I am president of Macalester College. What a humbling, exhilarating, and sometimes trying position it is. What gratitude I feel for having been granted the great privilege I enjoy.

Joe Gargery, the larger-than-life innocent in Dickens's *Great Expectations*, describes his relationship to Pip and to the world in a phrase that, like so much in Dickens, has no simple translation but captures a complex mixture of joy, wistfulness, and earned wisdom: "what larks!" I am inclined to say the same about the last ten years of my life. ■

—BRIAN ROSENBERG, November 2013

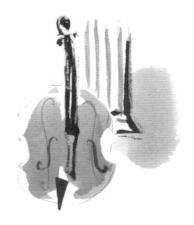

On the Importance of the Liberal Arts

Higher Education and Democracy

From *Macalester Today*, Fall 2006

"An educated citizenry is the essential instrument for promoting responsible social action and community well-being." —EUGENE LANG

This past June I was one of several American college presidents invited to attend a forum at the Council of Europe headquarters in Strasbourg, France, on "Higher Education and Democratic Culture: Citizenship, Human Rights and Civic Responsibility." (I know, I know, it's a tough job....) The purpose of the forum was to bring together leaders of colleges and universities in the United States and Europe—along with a few representatives from Asia and Australia—to "explore the responsibility of higher education for advancing sustainable democratic culture."

Several thoughts struck me during the course of the meeting. One is that American colleges and universities, for all our challenges and despite the obvious need to do better, are much further along than are our European counterparts in thinking about post-secondary education as preparation for engagement and responsible leadership in local, national, and global communities. We educate a larger and more diverse segment of our population in a larger and more diverse set of skills, and we make a more concerted effort to embed vocational preparation within the broader context of what might be termed preparation for citizenship.

Another thought is that American liberal arts colleges by and large define their responsibility to society in different terms than do American research universities: While the latter might identify their chief contribution as the production of important and original research (or at least organize their priorities *as if* this is their belief), the former would almost certainly identify that contribution as the production of what Frank Rhodes, President Emeritus of Cornell University, termed "a steady stream of informed, influential, and engaged graduates." Of course these missions overlap—research universities do produce such graduates, and the faculty at colleges such as Macalester do make significant contributions to scholarship—but the difference in emphasis is real and telling and may help explain why liberal arts college graduates appear, at least to those of us who pay attention to such things, to have a social impact disproportionate to their relatively small numbers.

The belief that informs liberal arts education in America is that democratic citizenship is best fostered not through indoctrination into the virtues of democracy, but through providing what Rhodes called the "essential equipment for the free and educated person" and through addressing what Brenda Gourley,

Vice Chancellor of Britain's Open University, called "the large issues and challenges of our time and place." In other words, democracy is best served not simply by teaching democracy, but by inculcating the skills, habits of mind, and knowledge without which effective democracy is impossible. This is by no means to say that courses in "American Government" or internships at the state capital are unimportant, any more than it would be unimportant for a student of literature to take courses in the "History and Theory of the Novel"; it is to say, however, that the former are insufficient to produce engaged citizens, just as the latter are insufficient to produce gifted novelists.

This is why courses in physics and painting, geology and classical Greek, are as essential as courses in politics and international studies to the creation of global citizens. They prepare the kinds of individuals—the minds, sensibilities, and characters—without which "sustainable democratic culture" is difficult if not impossible. They shape and inform the countless internships, volunteer jobs, and community-service positions occupied by our students. They strengthen in those students an appreciation of beauty, reason, open-mindedness, and rigorous thought. And this is why I continue to believe that maintaining a broad, diverse, and challenging curriculum is central to, even the bedrock of, the social mission of Macalester.

This is also why I believe that a widely accessible system of liberal education is a prerequisite for effective democracy. It is not enough to have the right statutes or structures in place; democracy in particular requires the participation of individuals prepared for both the challenges and opportunities of freedom. This preparation, in the words of the organizers of the Strasbourg forum, "encompasses democratic values, ways of knowing and acting, ethical judgments, analytical competencies, and skills of engagement." It includes "awareness of and concern for human rights as well as openness to the cultural diversity of human experience and a willingness to give due consideration to the views of others." In sum, preparation for the condition of freedom is the animating work within and beyond the classrooms, laboratories, and studios at Macalester.

Higher education indeed bears much responsibility for advancing sustainable democratic culture; the corollary, however, is that democratic societies bear much responsibility for supporting and strengthening higher education, and especially education in the liberal arts. This is a lesson underscored at least since the founding of our particular democracy, but of which we can never too often be reminded. ■

More Precious Than Rubies: The Purposes of Higher Education

Sermon delivered at House of Hope Presbyterian Church, St. Paul, February 4, 2007

I t is a deep pleasure for me to be here with all of you today and to share in the ceremonies of Macalester Sunday at House of Hope, an annual recognition of the conjoined histories of two institutions founded a century and a half ago by the Reverend Edward Duffield Neill, one of the pioneering leaders of education and worship in the Twin Cities. You will not be astonished to hear that I am also, to quote the great Romantic poet William Wordsworth, "surprised by joy"[1] on this occasion, since this pulpit is not a spot on which I could reasonably have been expected to stand. Like most of us, I imagined as a child—in my case as a child growing up in the suburbs of New York City—a panoply of future situations and challenges for myself: some more fantastic and some more far-fetched than others, particularly those involving center field, Yankee Stadium, and the World Series. I will confess that figuring as the featured speaker on a Sunday morning before a large and distinguished Presbyterian congregation in St. Paul, Minnesota, was never one of these. And yet here I am, and here you are, and we will together see what comes of it.

One thing that is not surprising, given that this is Macalester Sunday and that I have some fairly visible association with the college, is the subject of my remarks this morning, which is "education," or more precisely the "purposes of higher—or what is sometimes less elegantly referred to as 'post-secondary'—education," a subject to which I naturally devote a good deal of whatever thought remains after I perform the rest of my daily job. At first blush this topic might seem fairly straightforward, since education would be accepted by most people as an over-whelming good and its aims reasonably clear and certainly noble. I say "most people" because there are of course exceptions, such as G. K. Chesterton, who complained that "the purpose of compulsory education is to deprive the common people of their common sense,"[2] or Mark Twain, who observed that "soap and education are not as sudden as a massacre, but they are more deadly in the long run."[3] But, these eloquent cynics aside, education in general and higher education in particular are embraced by most civilized people as foundational characteristics of civilized society and as things eminently worth having.

Yet we find in even the most ancient and venerable writings about education no agreement about its goals, purposes, and desired outcomes. In the Book of Proverbs we are told that "Wisdom is supreme; therefore get wisdom./ Though it cost you all you have, get understanding" (4:7), and we are advised by wisdom to "Choose my instruction instead of silver,/knowledge

rather than choice gold,/for wisdom is more precious than rubies,/and nothing you desire can compare with her" (8:10-11).
At the same time we are told that "A wise man has great power,/
and a man of knowledge increases strength" (24:5), allowing for
a most interesting discussion about whether education should
be seen as an alternative or as a means to worldly wealth and accomplishment. Should education be designed to carry us away
from the practicalities of life toward some higher set of values
or should it prepare us for those practicalities and therefore for
security and even riches? Is education about wisdom and the
formation of character or is it about vocation and the development of abilities and skills? And to what extent are these different goals contradictory or compatible?

Among the great thinkers of antiquity and of American history we see similar tensions animating deliberations on how
best to educate young men—and eventually young women—
most beneficially. A number of historians have distinguished
between the Socratic emphasis on education as a process of
self-scrutiny— as essentially inward looking—and the Ciceronian tradition of education as preparation for the duties of citizenship—or as essentially outward looking.[4] Thomas Jefferson
and Benjamin Franklin, who in addition to their other noteworthy achievements were the founders respectively of the Universities of Virginia and Pennsylvania, shared a sense of the importance of higher education but differed somewhat in emphasis:
Jefferson focusing more on the relations between education
and democratic citizenship and Franklin on what he termed
"useful" things such as mathematics, accounting, and science.[5]
This tension was perpetuated through much of the nineteenth
century as youthful American universities and liberal arts colleges, most of them church founded or related, wrestled with
the question of whether their purpose was to form particular

kinds of people or to inculcate useful knowledge and critical and practical skills.

We see some of these same conflicts being played out today, perhaps most visibly through what has become known as the Spellings Commission Report, a document on the future of American higher learning prepared by a group under the direction of the Secretary of Education. The report opens with a statement entitled "The Value of Higher Education," which reads as follows:

> *In an era when intellectual capital is increasingly prized both for individuals and for the nation, postsecondary education has never been more important. Ninety percent of the fastest-growing jobs in the new knowledge-driven economy will require some postsecondary education. Already, the median earnings of a U.S. worker with only a high school diploma are 37 percent less than those of a worker with a bachelor's degree. Colleges and universities must continue to be the major route for new generations of Americans to achieve social mobility. And for the country as a whole, future economic growth will depend on our ability to sustain excellence, innovation, and leadership in higher education. But even the economic benefits of a college degree could diminish if students don't acquire the appropriate skills.*[6]

We are in this statement a long way from the Book of Proverbs and the counsel to "Choose my instruction instead of silver,/ knowledge rather than choice gold,/for wisdom is more precious than rubies,/and nothing you desire can compare with her." Indeed, if the report of the Spellings Commission is to be believed, the debate over the purposes of higher education has been settled once and for all and the answer is, to paraphrase an earlier Presidential campaign, "it's the economy, stupid."

Education in the report of the Spellings Commission, education in most of the public discourse in our state houses and in Washington, D.C., education in most of the meetings of chambers of commerce, education as discussed in most of our newspapers and on most of our talk shows, is conceived of chiefly in material and vocational terms: as an engine of personal and communal economic growth, as a tool for workforce development, and as a means of maintaining American competitiveness in an increasingly interconnected world. More and more often, educational systems such as the one now emerging in China are held up by policymakers as models of efficiency and national single-mindedness to which we should aspire.

Now, let me be absolutely clear about the fact that I believe this goal to be a good and important one. To educate students without providing the requisite tools for vocational and economic success and security is to abdicate a critical ethical and social responsibility. There is a difference, however, between being a *worthy* goal and being the *only* goal, and I fear that we are increasingly in danger of defining education, and especially higher education, entirely in terms of its vocational and economic role: in terms, as it were, of its ability to help us get and spend silver, rubies, and gold. Certainly this is and has been true in many parts of the world, including the aforementioned China, where hundreds and even thousands of new universities are being created, almost all of which emphasize career training in engineering, accounting, and other subjects that are seen as crucial to economic growth. Given the recent rate of expansion of China's economy, it would be difficult to argue with the near-term effectiveness of this strategy.

In the United States, by contrast, vocational preparation has historically been joined by at least two other central and interrelated goals for higher education: individual enlightenment and self-understanding, or what might idealistically be called the getting of wisdom, and preparation for engaged citizenship in a democratic society. From these other goals have developed the rich diversity and distinctive character of American colleges and universities: the range of public and private institutions, with their many different access points into post-secondary education; the liberal arts curriculum, with its focus on breadth as well as depth of knowledge; the residential college, with its encouragement of instructional opportunities both inside and outside the classroom; the commitment to civic engagement among students and faculty. And from these developments, in turn, have sprung so many of the economic, technological, and social accomplishments of this country and its longstanding (if newly threatened and precarious) position of global leadership. I would contend, that is, that our less narrowly focused, more diffuse, and in utilitarian terms more "inefficient" form of higher education in America has engendered the flexibility, creativity, and sense of collective responsibility that have been the drivers of the most successful and longest-lived experiment in democratic governance in the world.

My fear is that in our quest to redefine education as efficient vocational training and to emulate other educational systems around the world, we will willingly devalue or even abandon these other, more complex, and ultimately more challenging goals. Efficiency narrowly understood may come at the expense of effectiveness broadly conceived as the shaping of characters, cultures, and values. I do not believe that when Jefferson made his famous comment that "If a nation expects to be ignorant and free, in a state of civilization, it expects what never was and never will be,"[7] he was thinking merely about the state of the economy; nor do I think that Abraham Lincoln was thinking about vocational skills when he wrote that at least a "moderate education" was required for each of us to "duly appreciate the value of our free institutions." [8]

What does it mean to educate students for citizenship in a free society? Some answers to that question remain unchanged since the days of Jefferson and Lincoln: it means to provide them with the skills, habits of mind, and breadth of knowledge that allow for informed participation in democracy; it means inculcating an abiding respect for the humanity of others; it means teaching the nature and importance of the civil exchange of ideas, particularly around difficult issues; it means exposure to and analysis of the best and most beautiful—as well as the worst and most terrifying—that humankind has produced. Some answers to the question have changed: today, and more than ever, it means preparing students to engage with diverse communities and cultures within our cities and our country and around the world and equipping them to use and not be overwhelmed by the opportunities of new technologies. It means readying them to live on a planet whose population is increasingly urban, whose environment is increasingly at risk, and whose distribution of wealth and resources is increasingly uneven. It means doing more than encouraging them to think about the economic benefits of a college degree.

Of the three chief purposes of higher education—career training, self-enlightenment, and preparation for citizenship— it may ultimately be the third that is both the most difficult and the most important. It is the most difficult because it is the one goal of education that is not chiefly about the betterment of the self, to which we might naturally be inclined, but about the betterment of and service to others, toward which we might need to be encouraged and around which advanced civilizations must be built; it is the most important for precisely that same reason. If higher education can do one single thing well, I would have it be to teach us, in the words of Yale law professor Stephen L. Carter, to "come into the presence of our fellow human beings with a sense of awe and gratitude" and to "listen to others with knowledge of the possibility that they are right and we are wrong."[9] Put another way, and perhaps quixotically, it would teach us what the poet John Keats called "negative capability," or the ability to negate for a time our own perspectives and see the world through the eyes of others.[10]

I am convinced that if colleges do this they will ineluctably be educating the people who will work to quell the conflicts and lessen the inequities and reverse the environmental disasters of today because those people will not only know enough but *care* enough to do so. Perhaps not all of higher education, perhaps not even most of higher education, but some segment of higher education in America had better be pursuing this particular goal—a goal that is indeed in my view infinitely "more precious than rubies" and that truly makes higher education a higher calling—or we will be failing in our responsibility to ourselves, our children, and the world they will inherit. ∎

1   "Surprised by joy—impatient as the Wind," 1815.
2   *Illustrated London News*, 7 September 1929.
3   "Facts Concerning the Recent Resignation," 27 December 1867.
4   See Hugh Hawkins, "The Making of the Liberal Arts College Identity," *Distinctively American: The Residential Liberal Arts Colleges* (New Brunswick: Transaction Publishers, 2000), 4-5; and Bruce Kimball, *Orators & Philosophers: A History of the Idea of Liberal Education* (New York: Teachers College Press, 1986).
5   Franklin, "Proposals Related to the Education of Youth in Pennsylvania," 1749.
6   *A Test of Leadership: Charting the Future of U. S. Higher Education,* A Report of he Commission Appointed by Secretary of Education Margaret Spellings, September 2006, 1.
7   Thomas Jefferson to Charles Yancey, January 6, 1816, cited in William G. Bowen, Martin A. Kurzweil, and Eugene M. Tobin, *Equity and Excellence in American Higher Education* (Charlottesville: University of Virginia Press, 2005) 4.
8   First Political Announcement, 9 March 1832.
9   *Civility: Manners, Morals, and the Etiquette of Democracy* (New York: Basic Books, 1998), 102, 139.
10 Letter to George and Thomas Keats, 21 December 1817.

A Pause for Student Appreciation

From *Macalester Today,* Spring 2009

One of the more insidious effects of crises and disasters is their power to attenuate our appreciation of many things that remain good and important. Certainly this is true of the current economic crisis, which has, for very compelling reasons, left colleges and universities chiefly focused on their financial stability and made it more difficult to devote appropriate attention to the wondrous accomplishments and ambitions of our students. I want to make sure that this does not happen at Macalester. Even as we work with special diligence to safeguard the financial future of the college, we need to remind ourselves of *why* that future is worth preserving by noting and applauding the fruits of the education we provide.

So let us agree to take a momentary pause from the grinding work of balancing budgets to commend the efforts of Macalester students.

We should applaud the work of the students who have participated in the Projects for Peace Program, funded through the generosity of Kathryn Wasserman Davis. Among these is Dara Hoppe '10, who during the summer of 2007 traveled to the Brazilian Amazon, where she encouraged sustainable economic development and independence by providing training to women in handicrafts production and distribution. Zainab Mansaray '09 and Arthur Sillah '10, both from Sierra Leone, traveled home this past summer to rehabilitate a primary school destroyed in the recent war and to implement community service projects for youths on malaria prevention, HIV/AIDS awareness, and environmental sustainability.

We should honor the achievements of student scholars such as Michael Waul '09, who will use his Rhodes Scholarship to pursue a two-year degree in medicinal chemistry at Oxford University; Chris Ramon '08, who is using his Fulbright Scholarship to explore immigration law and workers' rights in Spain; and Hector Pascual Alvarez '08, who is using his Watson Fellowship to study the role of community-based theater in Latin America, South Africa, and the United Kingdom.

We should appreciate the dedication of Lilly Fellows such as Emily Cohen '09, Hannah Pallmeyer '09, and Hannah Emple '10. Emily worked with the St. Paul Area Council of Churches on interfaith engagement among Muslims, Christians, and Jews; Hannah Pallmeyer worked at the International Institute of Minnesota on refugee settlement and support; and Hannah Emple worked with Minnesota International Health Volunteers on issues relating to breast cancer among Somali women.

Jenna Machado '12 started a suicide prevention nonprofit in Colorado with the goal of preventing teen suicide by sending trained peer-mentors into the school system. She plans to create a similar program in St. Paul.

Phillips Scholarships are awarded to students who strive to make life better for people with unmet needs in Minnesota communities, and Elizabeth McCreary '09 used her scholarship to develop artistic and educational activities for homeless children. Elizabeth's work has also been recognized by the Jimmy and Rosalynn Carter Partnership Foundation.

The efforts among Macalester students to develop a higher level of environmental awareness and responsibility are almost too numerous to count. Timothy den Herder-Thomas '09 developed Summer of Solutions, a program for students from around the country created and run by students at Macalester. For two months last summer, these students gathered on our campus to learn how to foster our transformation to a more sustainable society, and during the coming summer the program will expand to include up to ten additional cities. MacCares, our student environmental organization, has worked with staff in Facilities Management and others on campus to begin to change in dramatic ways how we live on campus—and to save us money in the process.

It would not be an exaggeration to suggest that I could expand this list to fill an entire issue of *Macalester Today*. Students at Macalester in every year, from every field of study, and with a wide range of interests and priorities are combining their dedication to learning with a passion for improving life on campus, in our local community, and beyond. They are the ones with the skills and motivation to take up the many challenges with which we are currently faced. They are the reasons why we must, in the near term, overcome those challenges and ensure that the critically important work of education, at Macalester and throughout the world, moves forward. ■

The Hidden Beauty of the World

From *Macalester Today,* Fall 2009

I have come to believe that there are few truths about the world we inhabit that were not spoken in some form by the great writers of the nineteenth century. (Full disclosure: I am hopelessly biased by the fact that I devoted a good portion of my life to reading, studying, and teaching precisely those writers.) Take, as an example, the question of the centrality of the fine arts—music, visual art, theater, and dance—to a liberal arts education of the highest quality. I can write with some clarity and much conviction about the value of appreciating beauty and about the ability of the non-verbal arts in particular to transcend cultural boundaries and bring disparate parts of the globe closer together. But, in reality, I can do no better than to point to the insights of my much more articulate Romantic and Victorian predecessors.

In his dramatic monologue "Fra Lippo Lippi," Robert Browning assumes the voice of a Renaissance painter and writes that "we're made so that we love/ First when we see them painted, things we have passed/ Perhaps a hundred times nor cared to see;/ and so they are better, painted—better to us,/ Which is the same thing. Art was given for that." Browning is writing about the process of what later critics came to call *defamiliarization* or *estrangement:* the ability of art of make the world around us appear unfamiliar and fresh and thereby to renew and intensify sensation. In effect, some would argue, we would without great art lose the ability to perceive and appreciate the world in all its fullness. The repetition and overstimulation of daily life cloud our perception; art acts as a restorative antidote.

Stated more concretely, we are being reminded that a great painted landscape or portrait has the power to make us see (or re-see) the contours of the physical world or the human form; that an aria movingly sung or a ballet gracefully performed reminds us of the human capacity for beauteous action; that *King Lear* or *Angels in America* reawakens us to the limits of our endurance and our ability to draw strength from suffering. To paraphrase Percy Shelley, great art "lifts the veil from the hidden beauty of the world, and makes familiar objects be as if they were not familiar."

Still more important, perhaps, is the ability of the arts to create and strengthen an empathic response to the people and events around us: to allow us, even for an instant, to see the world through the eyes of others. The concept of empathy was first defined by German theorists in the 19th century, though it is captured most precisely, in my view, by the English poet John Keats, who wrote that "if a sparrow comes before my window I take part in its existence and pick about the gravel." It is Keats who coined the famous term "negative capability," by which, I believe, he meant the ability of the great artist temporarily to negate the self and understand the world from an alternative perspective—and, by extension, to allow the reader or viewer or listener to do the same. Even instrumental music, which is not mimetic and tells no literal story, generates at its best what researchers have described as an empathetic connection to a "mood [or] an emotional quality" that may be even more powerful than language.[1]

Any list of the abilities that should be inculcated by a first-rate liberal arts education would surely include near the very top both the capacity to *see* the world clearly, honestly, and with appreciation for its beauty, and the desire and capacity to *empathize* with the world view of those who are unlike ourselves. Indeed, it would not be difficult to argue that a good number of the difficulties we currently face are the result of the widespread absence of these abilities. We have suffered collectively from an absence of clear vision and an even more profound absence of empathic understanding. To the extent that the fine arts develop and enhance these critical dimensions of our humanity, they are essential to the education that colleges such as Macalester should provide: as essential as our commitment to bringing a diverse group of students to our community and to inspiring in them an abiding sense of social responsibility.

I suppose there is a rather straightforward syllogism that captures all of this. Vision and empathy—each of which is strengthened by exposure to and participation in the arts—are essential qualities for our leaders of the future. It is the responsibility of Macalester to educate those leaders. Therefore we at Macalester should keep the arts at the center of our work.

Simple. ■

---

[1] Laura Brester, "The Music Lesson," *Handbook of the Arts in Qualitative Research*, ed. J. Gary Knowles and Ardra L. Cole (Thousand Oaks, Calif.: Sage, 2007) 230.

Will Dropouts Save America? No.

From *The Huffington Post,* October 27, 2011

I want to begin by congratulating Michael Ellsberg, who this past Sunday published in the pages of *The New York Times* an op-ed piece ("Will Dropouts Save America?") arguing that the key to America's economic future was the production of more college dropouts. Somehow he managed to skip the marketing section of *The Times* altogether and publish an extended advertisement for his book, *The Education of Millionaires: It's Not What You Think and It's Not Too Late,* for free. Nicely done.

There are few things more condescending and destructive than those who have benefited from an expensive and intensive college education (Mr. Ellsberg is a graduate of Brown University) arguing that others need not bother about such benefits for themselves.

Let us take a look at Mr. Ellsberg's argument. "Certainly, if you want to become a doctor, lawyer, or engineer, then you must go to college." "True, people with college degrees tend to earn more." "…most people who end up starting businesses likely have college degrees…" One would think that these would together comprise a reasonably compelling case for the benefits to our society and our economy of *fewer* dropouts.

But if you reach such a conclusion, you have probably had your creative thinking crushed by such unnecessary college courses as economics, statistics, and philosophy (where they teach logic). Mr. Ellsberg takes us down a different road.

Yes, colleges are good at producing "professionals with degrees." But, he counters, "we don't have a shortage of lawyers and professors." Leaving aside the question of whether we will benefit in the future from well-educated lawyers and professors, I note that Mr. Ellsberg fails here to mention doctors or engineers or researchers or any other professionals in fields related to science and mathematics, where we do in fact face a dangerous shortage in the United States and upon whom global health, global innovation, and the global economy are so dependent.

People with college degrees do indeed earn more—and find jobs more easily, with an unemployment rate at present in this country of about 5 percent—but, Mr. Ellsberg insists, "there is little evidence to suggest that the same ambitious people would earn less without college degrees (particularly if they mastered true business and networking grit)." There is little evidence because there *cannot by definition* be such evidence: it is simply impossible to prove a hypothetical negative of this kind. I leave it to the reader to determine whether or not "grit" sounds like a reasonable alternative to a better system of science education for America's youth.

As for the detail that most business creators have college degrees? Mr. Ellsberg is prepared for that one as well. "Assuming that college was responsible for their success gives higher education more credit than it deserves." Here as elsewhere, Mr. Ellsberg is describing and then attacking a straw man of his own creation. Few sensible people have ever argued that a college education is solely responsible for the success of talented and motivated individuals; rather, it seems reasonable to argue that a sound education is an important constituent part of the basis for that success.

In preparation for writing his book, Mr. Ellsberg "spent the last two years interviewing college dropouts who went on to become millionaires and billionaires." I presume that he did not interview college graduates who achieved similar financial success because the list was so much longer. His method also begs the question of whether college dropouts are the best source of reliable information about the nature and value of a college education.

So, what did he learn from these interviews?

Well, "our current classrooms…stifle creativity. If a young person happens to retain enough creative spirit to start a business upon graduation, she does so in spite of her schooling, not because of it." "From kindergarten through undergraduate and grad school, you learn very few skills or attitudes that would ever help you start a business. Skills like sales, networking, creativity and comfort with failure." I especially like the kindergarten reference: let's get those blocks and crayons out of those classrooms and begin working on eye contact (about which Mr. Ellsberg wrote an earlier book) and a firm handshake.

It's hard to know where to begin in responding to these contentions—that tends to be the case when contentions are based on no evidence—but I want at least to draw attention to

Mr. Ellsberg's arguments about creativity, which he appears to believe is an inherent quality that is only diminished by excessive amounts of classroom time. Has he ever been in a lively classroom working with a gifted teacher? I am both a parent and a college president, and I have seen firsthand that the creative abilities of both my children and the students at my institution are far more often enhanced than stifled by the study of art and literature, the pursuit of answers in a laboratory, or a deeper understanding of human history and psychology. To Mr. Ellsberg these are merely "narrowly defined academic subjects"—as opposed to more practical skills, I would assume, in such areas as sales and networking.

Arguments like Mr. Ellsberg's might simply be dismissed as silly, but these days they are, unhappily, more likely than ever to foster the spread of misinformation and to be used as the basis for terrible public-policy proposals. It remains the case that there is not a single example of a society in this or any other age that has improved its economy or strengthened its civic institutions by educating fewer of its people. That isn't as catchy as offering seven easy steps toward becoming a millionaire or billionaire without a college degree (that's the number in Mr. Ellsberg's book), but it is true. Mr. Ellsberg ends by noting that, "I'd put my money on the kids who are dropping out of colleges to start new businesses." Unfortunately the opposite is true: in marketing his *Education of Millionaires,* he is *taking* the money of such kids (only $14.99 for the Kindle edition) and delivering to young people who are working hard to get an education exactly the wrong message. ■

What Higher Education Can Learn from Steve Jobs

From *The Huffington Post,* November 9, 2011

Steve Jobs was not a nice man: this is made abundantly clear by Walter Isaacson's compelling new biography of the former leader of Apple. He was, however, almost preternaturally insightful about such things as the nature of the creative process, the relationship between a product and its user, and the need for balance between complexity and simplicity.

There are lessons in Jobs's success that are I believe directly relevant to higher education, though they may not be the most obvious ones. Whether or not the iPad will replace the traditional textbook or distance learning will increasingly displace the traditional classroom I cannot say (though I suspect the answer in both cases is "yes"). The lessons to which I refer, however, are more fundamental and touch upon how higher education imagines itself today and in the future. Three of Jobs's particular insights have stuck with me since I finished reading the story of his life.

"Deciding what not to do is as important as deciding what to do."

One of Jobs's first major decisions when he returned to Apple in 1997 was to reduce the number of products the company made at a time when most technology companies were expanding their product lines. He believed that the future success of the company was dependent upon doing a few things supremely well, as opposed to doing many things pretty well, and that those two approaches were incompatible.

One of higher education's great weaknesses is the inability to decide what *not* to do. We see this played out in many ways: on a curricular level, where the proliferation of programs without the proliferation of resources makes it very difficult to maintain high quality across the board; on an institutional level, particularly at research universities, where the attempt simultaneously to educate undergraduates and graduate students, to run a hospital and a law school, and to field semi-professional football and basketball teams creates entities that are sprawling, disconnected, and poorly focused. We see it within consortia of colleges, where redundancies are created because it is easier to avoid deciding what not to do than to increase educational efficiency.

There would be sufficient variety and capacity within the American higher education system to do many things supremely well if we were willing to distinguish the essential from the ancillary, to try less often to be all things to all people, and, at least from time to time, to decide what not to do. Instead we seem to have settled into a system of doing many things pretty well, and I'm not sure that will be good enough.

*"Some people say, 'Give the customers what they want.'
But that's not my approach. Our job is to figure out what
they're going to want before they do."*

Jobs goes on to quote Henry Ford: "If I'd asked customers what they wanted, they would have told me, 'A faster horse!'"

There are far too many people these days who are asking higher education to produce a faster horse: who are, that is, making judgments about the ideal future for higher education chiefly on the basis of their perception of the present and without any serious attempt to imagine and prepare for the future. They are insisting that the "customer" knows best and that the job of higher education is simply, as the popular phrase goes, to give the people what they want.

As is often the case with erroneous arguments, this one contains a germ of truth. Higher education needs to be seriously attentive to the needs of the work force and to the desires of those who are the recipients of their services. We have not been as attentive to these things as we should be.

But being attentive does not mean being mechanically responsive, and if all higher education does is respond to external prescriptions, it will be failing in one of its central responsibilities.

It is in no way demeaning to say that students are called students because they still have things to learn, and that the responsibility of higher education is to figure out—working in concert with many other groups—what those things should be. It is frankly preposterous for someone who has never taken a college course in anthropology or philosophy to declare that those courses have no value.

It is equally preposterous to idealize an educational system that would be entirely focused on the vocational skills that are most necessary in the year 2011. Of course we must teach those skills, and we must teach them to more students than we do at present. But we must also try to anticipate the skills that will be most necessary in 2021 and 2031 and to teach the habits of mind that will enable graduates to adapt and adjust as the world, and the economy, changes around them. It is chiefly the responsibility of the faculties of colleges and universities to make these determinations.

> *"The creativity that can occur when a feel for both the humanities and the sciences combine in one strong personality was the topic that most interested me in the biographies of Franklin and Einstein, and I believe that it will be a key to creating innovative economies in the twenty-first century."*

Jobs described the intersection of the humanities and the sciences as "magical," and he distinguished between Apple and Microsoft by asserting (rightly or wrongly I cannot say) that "Microsoft never had the humanities and liberal arts in its DNA."

So let me be clear. Yes, we need more scientists and more engineers. Yes, we need more people with the high-level vocational skills required for a knowledge economy. But we *also* need some meaningful number of people who are liberally educated, that is, who are educated broadly and deeply in areas of the arts and humanities that are too often considered impractical.

It is a mistake to believe that one can reliably imagine the future without studying the past, as one does through the discipline of history. It is a mistake to believe that one can create beautiful and useful products without some engagement with fields such as art and music, where the human capacity for creativity is so spectacularly on display. It is a mistake to believe that one can form the empathy necessary to engage fully with the world's problems without developing what the poet John Keats called "negative capability," or the ability to step out of oneself that comes with the reading and study of literature.

If we are in fact to create an innovative economy for this and future centuries, we need someplace in our system of higher education for that "magical" intersection of multiple disciplines and perspectives that is central to the liberal arts.

Such an education might not be the right prescription for everyone, but unless it is available to those whose imaginations it excites, our system of higher education will be greatly diminished. Steve Jobs, in one of his milder moments, would have called an educational system devoid of the liberal arts, like a computer or a phone or a music player devoid of both beauty and functionality, "a piece of crap." I can't say that I disagree. ∎

For Their Own Good

A version of this essay was published in *The Chronicle of Higher Education*, July 26, 2012.

P eter Wood, President of the National Association of Scholars (NAS), is a skilled writer with a quick wit. His latest article on American higher education, "Helium, Part 2," published in *The Chronicle of Higher Education*, deftly weaves together a variety of the favorite targets of the NAS—government funding of higher education, lack of "rigor" in colleges, President Obama, the decline of "college curricula rooted in the civilization that has sustained the university for more than a millennium," radicalized college faculties, complacent college administrators, the failure of traditional institutions to embrace on-line instruction—into a single and supremely self-assured narrative of imminent collapse.

Maybe Dr. Wood is right about all of this. I hope not, but then, as he would be quick to point out, I am, as the president of a liberal arts college, deeply invested in the system that he believes to be on the verge of a self-created collapse. The last time I attempted to defend higher education, against the attacks of the erstwhile presidential candidate Rick Santorum, Dr. Wood accused me in *The Chronicle* of "contumely." I am learning to live with this burden.

One statement near the end of Dr. Wood's latest piece, however, cannot be allowed to stand without comment.

> *"Too many students are going to college—too many for their own good, but also too many for the good of college itself."*

Here Dr. Wood joins a list of other college-educated figures—including Senator Santorum, billionaire Peter Thiel, and author Michael Ellsberg—who contend that others are not in need of the sort of educational advantage that they themselves received. This has become something of a drumbeat in recent months.

Currently in the United States, 39 percent of adults aged 35 to 64 are holders of an associate's degree or higher. The percentage of adults aged 25 to 34 who are holders of an associate's degree or higher is...39 percent. To provide some context, the comparable figures for Canada are 44 and 55 percent; for Japan, 35 and 54 percent; for Korea, 25 and 53 percent. For the older demographic, the United States ranks second to Canada in higher education attainment; for the younger demographic, the United States ranks tenth among developed nations. In other words, the rest of the world is getting more educated more quickly than is the U.S.

> *"Too many students are going to college—too many for their own good..."*

According to the Bureau of Labor Statistics, the unemployment rate from 2001 to 2010 among those with a bachelor's degree averaged 2.9 percent. The rate among those with a high school degree averaged 5.9 percent. The May 2012 national unemployment rate stood at 8.2 percent; the rate among those with a bachelor's degree was 4.1 percent. In a recent commentary in *Bloomberg News* that is anything but a puff piece for higher education, A. Gary Shilling reports that "those lacking a high-school diploma average $973,000 [in lifetime earnings] in 2009 dollars and advanced-degree holders can expect to make $3 million or more during their careers."

The students least well served by our educational system are those who come from the least affluent backgrounds, and those are also the students for whom higher education provides the greatest advantage. According to the Pew Charitable Trusts, 62 percent of children from the bottom income quintile who attain a college degree escape poverty, compared with less than a third of those without a college degree.

According, again, to the Bureau of Labor Statistics, states with higher levels of educational attainment see higher wages for *all* categories of workers, including those without college degrees. Wages for those with only high-school degrees are 27 percent higher in the states with high levels of college attainment than in those with low levels. In other words, more education means better jobs and more prosperity for entire communities, not simply for the degree-holders.

In my own state of Minnesota, I have for the past year been part of a task force devoted to the improvement of higher education in the state. This has been a business–education partnership, with participation from the leaders of many of the largest employers in the state. Here is a passage from the group's recently published report: "Higher education is central to supplying the skilled talent and innovations that are major drivers of productivity and job creation. Therefore, it is essential that Minnesota continues to promote an exemplary higher education system." This comes from the leadership of companies including Cargill, Target, General Mills, and U.S. Bank—not from higher education itself, and not from those who are unfamiliar with the needs of the marketplace.

It is neither unusual nor surprising when those in possession of something of great value, like a college degree, suggest that others less fortunate would, "for their own good," be better off without that valuable possession. It is also condescending and, sometimes, destructive. We need more Americans, not fewer, to have easier and more affordable access to higher education. For our failures in this area higher education must bear some of the blame, as must public officials who have systematically disinvested in higher education over an extended period of time and those who are spreading the gospel of education for fewer.

Among the profound ironies of the current anti-education argument is that it is not in fact "rooted in the civilization that has sustained the university for more than a millennium" and whose devaluing the NAS and others lament. Much has been written about the commitment to a broadly educated populace of Thomas Jefferson and Benjamin Franklin and about their belief in the interdependence of education and democracy. And it was John Adams who wrote in 1785 that, "The whole people must take upon themselves the education of the whole people and be willing to bear the expenses of it."

Perhaps we can all benefit from spending more time this summer reading the Founding Fathers. ∎

Creativity

From *The Huffington Post,* December 7, 2012

Sir Ken Robinson's TEDTalk on "Schools Killing Creativity" is enormously entertaining and so rousing that one feels sheepish about questioning any of its parts. Of course, he begins with the dual advantage of being very funny and very British, a combination that audiences in America, at least, tend to find irresistible.

He also operates on a level of generality that brooks almost no opposition. Who, after all, is against creativity? (Well, perhaps certain members of the United States Congress, but we will leave that for another column.) Who does not wish to see our children flourish? Who can resist a good joke at the expense of college professors, who make such delicious targets? His line about faculty members treating their bodies as vehicles to carry their heads from meeting to meeting is one that I can assure you I will steal.

Sir Ken—another advantage of being British is the opportunity to be called things like "Sir Ken"—makes what is essentially a Romantic argument about the inherent creativity of children and the tendency of schools and other social institutions gradually and inexorably to stifle those creative impulses. This is the argument made by Rousseau in *The Social Contract,* which begins with the famous observation that "Man is born free, and everywhere he is in chains." It is the central premise of Wordsworth's "Ode: Intimations of Immortality," in which he laments that "Shades of the prison-house begin to close/ Upon the growing boy" as he matures. It is among the main subjects of Dickens's *Hard Times,* whose villain Mr. Gradgrind declares, "Facts. Teach these boys and girls nothing but Facts. Facts alone are wanted in life"—only to be proven disastrously wrong through the ruination of his own daughter.

Mostly I agree with Sir Ken's contention that school systems around the world are in their structure and curricula biased in favor of what we think of as left-brain activities like mathematics and language-use and are too quick to dismiss, or even diagnose as pathologies, many of the creative activities associated with the right-brain. Among the negative effects of this bias are the rapidly rising number of students who arrive at colleges like my own on medications to treat behavioral disorders and, more broadly, the growing belief that education generally, and higher education in particular, can justify their existence (and their cost) only by providing very narrowly defined vocational training.

Here is what I think it is important to add to Sir Ken's description of the current state of education. First, the impact of the bias he describes is not evenly distributed. Here as elsewhere throughout our educational system, the negative effects are felt most powerfully by those who are most economically disadvantaged. Children who are fortunate enough to attend private schools or well-funded public schools in affluent neighborhoods may not be utterly free of socially imposed stifling, but they do in fact get the opportunity to dance and act and draw and sing both inside and outside of the classroom: perhaps not as often as might be ideal, but more often than most students in most places at most times in history.

For the many children who are not so fortunate, however, those opportunities are limited and diminishing in number. I do not think this is because second-grade teachers in public schools are, as Sir Ken seems to suggest, looking to educate future college professors. I think it is because they are provided with neither the time nor the resources to include in their curricula creative activities whose importance they generally recognize.

Second, I would feel more enthusiastic about encouraging right-brain activities if we were doing a better job with the stuff on the left. If, that is, our school systems were churning out legions of math and language masters, it would a little easier to imagine lessening our emphasis on such things as addition and grammar. But all evidence suggests that we are pretty bad and getting worse at providing our children with quantitative and linguistic skills that are essential whether one will be working in a bank or running a dance company. As long as we understand the nurturing of creativity as something our schools do *in addition to* rather than *instead of* teaching children to be comfortable with numbers and words, I am all for it.

Finally, I am not sure whether it was Sir Ken or the TED folks who entitled his presentation "Schools Killing Creativity," but if were up to me I would change it, perhaps to something like "Society Killing the Ability for Schools to Encourage Creativity," though I confess that this is much less catchy. It is easy and tempting to blame teachers or unions or self-absorbed professors for the problems in our educational system, but the reality is that here—as in the political institutions about which we so passionately complain—we get what we deserve, or rather, we get the natural result of the choices we make. Congress would not be such a disaster if we did not elect those people. Schools would not fail so regularly in fostering creativity if we did not make the choices we do through our school boards and selection of funding priorities and, most broadly, in how we choose as a society to allocate our resources.

As long as we keep spending more on armies than on education, it is going to be pretty darn hard to encourage more children to dance. ■

Ignorance about Education

From *The Huffington Post*, January 30, 2013

Ignorance has many powerful advantages over knowledge. Typically it is simple and easy to communicate, while knowledge, by its very nature, usually tends to be nuanced and complex. Ignorance requires no evidence and no research. It can be endlessly repeated and rapidly spread. It inflames passions. Its pervasiveness wears down those who attempt to combat it. And, often, it seems so outlandish and so—well, so *ignorant*—that it tends to be dismissed and underestimated by those in a position to know better: until it begins to take hold and become a kind of orthodoxy, by which point the damage is very hard to undo.

Which brings me to North Carolina Governor Patrick McCrory. Appearing on a radio program hosted by the indefatigable

Bill Bennett, who has mastered the art of replacing evidence with polemic, Governor McCrory said the following: "I'm looking at legislation right now—in fact, I just instructed my staff yesterday to go ahead and develop legislation—which would change the basic formula in how education money is given out to our universities and our community colleges.… It's not based on butts in seats but on how many of those butts can get jobs."

Then he dove thoughtfully into specifics: "If you want to take gender studies that's fine, go to a private school and take it.… But I don't want to subsidize that if that's not going to get someone a job." Asked by Bennett (who has a PhD, in philosophy, from a subsidized public university), "How many PhDs in philosophy do I need to subsidize?", Governor McCrory responded, "You and I agree," by which he presumably meant about the foolishness of subsidizing the study of philosophy, though I suspect the areas of agreement are considerably broader.

(Excuse me for a moment while I pause to breathe deeply.)

I so wish I lived in a world in which remarks of this kind could be called out as ignorant and summarily dismissed. But I don't, and they can't, and those of us who actually rely on evidence and information and who choose to remain silent in the face of remarks of this kind are complicit in the dumbing down of our public discourse and the failures of our public policy.

Governor McCrory's remarks are based on the following unsubstantiated assumptions: that public education has as its sole purpose in a democracy the preparation for a job; that one can predict based upon a student's area of study the employability and career path of that student; that one can know today where the jobs will be in ten or twenty years; that the skills most necessary for the generation of economic success and strong civil society in the 21st century are only taught in certain fields, which can be identified in advance and therefore appropriately funded by legislators; that the current public investment in an institution like the University of North Carolina is, in its present form, a bad one. This is not an exhaustive list, but it will do.

Here is what the evidence actually suggests about these assumptions: they are, in order, wrong, wrong, wrong, wrong, and wrong. On the plus side, they are simple, easy to communicate, and able to get a large number of people riled up.

Of course there are areas in which shortages of appropriately educated workers are harming our economy and our global competitiveness. Some of these require more robust vocational programs within our technical and community colleges, some require the encouragement and support of more students in disciplines such as engineering, computer science, and the life sciences. But it is also more true than ever before that students with a post-secondary education, regardless of major, will on average face lower levels of unemployment and achieve higher levels of income than those without a college degree; that many more graduates will change careers than will remain in the particular career for which their major initially prepared them; that many employers place the highest premium on skills such as critical thinking, creativity, and the ability to work cooperatively, in which a liberal arts education has been shown to provide especially good training; and that public investment in education, at all levels, has a better Return on Investment (ROI) than virtually any other investment a state or a nation can make.

It is also true that, on a per capita basis, liberal arts colleges send the most students into graduate training in those STEM disciplines—science, technology, engineering, mathematics—where jobs are most needed and from which economic growth is most likely to spring. So there seems to be a direct rather than an inverse correlation between being educated in an intellectually broad environment and economic prosperity. The butts in these seats find work. (Do not blame me for the image.)

If Governor McCrory has any evidence that any of these statements is untrue, I would be happy to examine it. I would be remiss in not acknowledging that there is one powerful piece of evidence to support the argument that a liberal arts education can be unhelpful in developing both judgment and job skills. Governor McCrory is himself a graduate of a liberal arts college with majors in political science and education.

No system is perfect. ■

Virtually Together

Sermon delivered at House of Hope Presbyterian Church, St. Paul, February 3, 2013

Good morning. It is a pleasure and a privilege to be with you on Macalester Sunday and to have been asked to speak for the second time from this rather imposing pulpit. I must confess that it always puts me in mind of the scene in the film version of *Moby Dick* in which Orson Welles, playing a bearded preacher, ascends a towering pulpit built from the prow of a ship and thunders at his congregation about Jonah and the whale. Clearly I am neither bearded nor a preacher nor very good at thundering, and I have no intention of talking about either Jonah or whales, but I will certainly, at least for the next few minutes, be towering.

Being here also puts me in mind of the inexorable passage of time. When I last assumed the role of preacher in this place, in

February of 2007, my two sons were boys. Now they are young men. My house was inhabited by four, and now on most days it is inhabited by two. I had yet to congratulate my fourth class of graduates at Macalester, and this May I will congratulate my tenth. The Colts were hours away from defeating the Bears 29 to 17 in the Super Bowl. Lehman Brothers and Borders existed and the iPhone and Twitter did not. Sandy Hook was just an elementary school, Gabby Giffords had just begun to serve her first term in the United States Congress, and Aurora, Colorado was perhaps best known for its selection by *Sports Illustrated* as one of America's great sports towns. And, in the unlikely event that you have forgotten, my topic that day was the meaning and importance of higher education.

This morning in 2013 my topic is different.

I have in recent months been prompted by occasions of loss and deep sadness to think more and more about the nature of community. It has been my impression that these months have seen an unusually high number of those I care about grow ill or pass away or be felled to their knees by sensations of overwhelming grief. Some of this, I know, is a consequence of my own aging and the inevitable aging of close friends and acquaintances by which it is accompanied. But aging does not explain the loss at the start of the school year of a nineteen-year-old Macalester exchange student in an accident only a mile from where we sit, or more recently the almost inconceivable loss of the beautiful twenty-year-old daughter of friends and colleagues in an accident on the other side of the world. To me, nothing explains such things.

For many of us, grief begets reflection about those concepts that are most profound and elusive: love and faith, fairness and chance, friendship and family. And I have indeed thought at one moment or another about each of these things. But I keep returning to the subject of community, perhaps because it has become so frequent a topic of discussion in my own particular professional sphere and because I have become so distressed at signs of breakdowns in community that threaten many of the things in which I most passionately believe. Turn on the television, if you must; watch the news, if you dare; and ask yourself if we appear to be creating the kinds of communities in which we want our children and grandchildren to live. Ask yourself if the fact that we can be exposed to more information more rapidly and make our thoughts public with the click of a mouse or the touch of a screen has made us behave with more wisdom and civility than did our parents. Ask yourself if the fact that we can now so easily find groups of like-minded individuals has made it more or less likely that we will empathize with those whose perspectives are different from our own.

It is both easy and tempting to imagine and even celebrate a future in which technology will allow us to do away with many of the norms of direct personal contact that have long established the basis of community. We no longer need to be on the same continent, let alone in the same room, to have face-to-face conversations. We no longer need even to have met someone to consider him or her a "friend" as that term has been redefined by new forms of social media. If we telecommute, we no longer need to be in a room with our coworkers, and if we take an online course we no longer need to be in a room with a teacher. We can shop without seeing a salesperson. We can speak volumes, and all too often we can shout, while concealing our identities beneath avatars and usernames and aliases. We can in fact move daily through an entire world without experiencing what would have been defined only twenty years ago as direct human contact. One could make a credible case that the nature of community has changed more fundamentally during the past two decades than during the previous two millennia. When I began my own academic career not so very long ago, there was no "e" in front of the word "mail."

Please know that there is much to admire and embrace within this brave new world. I love the fact that I was able to see my older son from the comfort of my living room while he was studying abroad in France. I love doing my Christmas shopping in my pajamas. I am in awe of the new, deep forms of learning that are being created at Macalester through the imaginative use of technology by brilliant teachers and scholars. I am humbled by the ability of students at my college to manage and manipulate information in ways I cannot even begin to comprehend. I very recently returned from a trip to Silicon Valley, where I visited Macalester alumni at the headquarters of Facebook and Google and came away deeply impressed not only by their brilliance, but by their deep commitment to making the world a better place. There is both wonder and a sense of inevitability in what we see unfolding so rapidly around us.

But while there is much here to inspire excitement, there is also much, I think, about which to be cautious. Technology has the power to expand and democratize knowledge and services and to make essentials like health care and education available to millions for whom they are now out of reach. In that sense it has the power to create a more just and prosperous global community. But, I fear, it also has the power to reinforce current inequalities and to create new ones.

In this country, and especially and sadly in Minnesota, there are enormous and growing disparities that threaten our prosperity and our civic life: disparities that begin with educational opportunity and expand to include income, health, safety, freedom, and hope. I have gone so far as to describe the existence of two Minnesotas: the one most of us in the room get to experience and the one being experienced daily by many who live only blocks away.

While technology has the power to weave these two Minnesotas closer together and to eliminate many of the differences, it also has the power to pull them further apart. It is not difficult to imagine a future in which those with means attend colleges like Macalester, rich above all with human contact, and those without means get taught on-line; in which those with means visit the doctor's office and those without receive medical advice on-line without ever hearing the voice of, let alone meeting with, a physician; perhaps even one in which those with means worship in beautiful sanctuaries like House of Hope and those without become part of virtual spiritual communities.

The same tools, in other words, that have the power to reduce inequities also have the power to increase them. The difference between these two outcomes lies not in the tools themselves but in the determination and goals of those of us who wield them. We will decide whether technology shrinks or expands the yawning gulf between the most and least fortunate in our state, our country, and our world. We will decide whether technology strengthens or dissipates community. We will decide whether reality becomes a luxury good.

I referred at the start of my remarks to moments of grief and deep sadness. Such moments, experienced alone, are nearly unendurable. So in healthy communities we gather together to experience them with others, to provide comfort and begin the process of healing, knowing all the while that healing may never be complete. Why do we do this? It is, I think, because the touch of an actual hand, the look of caring in an actual eye, are what define us as human. "Stable communities," according to Kurt Vonnegut, are places in which "the terrible disease of loneliness can be cured." [1] Both those who are experiencing grief and those who are providing comfort are vulnerable to that disease, and both draw strength from the curative power of gathering together. And such power is not confined to times of sadness, but is equally necessary at times of great joy. Thus we also gather together to celebrate births and marriages and graduations: to sing, to dance, to cry out with pleasure. There are few forms of loneliness more profound than experiencing joy alone.

Wendell Berry has written the following: "I believe that the community—in the fullest sense: a place and all its creatures—is the smallest unit of health and that to speak of the health of an isolated individual is a contradiction in terms."[2] The question for all of us to consider is whether the new virtual communities we are creating are indeed units of health. My honest answer is, I don't know. We know that such communities are larger and faster and cheaper. To build an on-line college or an on-line church would cost a small fraction of what it would cost to build a campus or a cathedral. This does matter. But at what cost do we purchase these savings? Nate Silver, our first celebrity statistician, has found evidence that when people hold strongly partisan beliefs, *more* information actually leads to *less* agreement.[3] Information, with which technology provides us in abundance, is not enough in itself to create community. Such creation requires that we interact in ways that break down the barriers that our beliefs incline us to construct and that the information we choose selectively to absorb is likely only to reinforce.

I am the president of the kind of college whose time, in the view of some, is soon to pass: a place of physical classrooms, green spaces, an actual library, rooms where people gather together to eat and play and talk. That access to such a place has become so expensive is a problem, and that so few young people get to experience such a place is unfair. But is the answer to this unfairness the elimination of some of the most enriching and inspiring settings the human imagination can create? It seems appropriate on this Macalester Sunday for me to say that the fundamental value of the college lies in its bringing together people from all over the country and all over the world to create a community whose bonds are strong and lasting. In such a community we learn better, we live better, we undergo a more profound transformation, than we would alone. Perhaps this will one day be supplanted by a world of massive open online courses, each of us gazing in solitude at screens in his or her own study. Our teachers, our classmates, and our friends will be measurable in pixels. If so, something of great value will have passed away. I hope we can create a future in which places such as Macalester are preserved but made more affordable and accessible through the great technological tools with which the human mind continues to provide us.

Allow me to offer you one last quotation, from Henry David Thoreau. "I have heard," Thoreau wrote, "of a man lost in the woods and dying of famine and exhaustion at the foot of a tree, whose loneliness was relieved by the grotesque visions with which, owing to bodily weakness, his diseased imagination surrounded him, and which he believed to be real. So also, owing to bodily and mental health and strength, we may be continually cheered by a like but more normal and natural society, and come to know that we are never alone." [4]

Now, I do not believe that the version of community we experience virtually is either grotesque or diseased, though at times one might think so from reading some of the anonymous comments posted after articles and blogs. But I do believe that such communities are to real human contact as visions are to reality. They are a simulacrum, a likeness. Like visions they can be beautiful or frightening, instructive or distracting. Like visions they come at nothing like the cost of actual experience.

But like visions they are in the end bodiless, and the fulfillment they provide is fleeting. Like the visions of the man in Thoreau's tale, they can sustain us when no actual human contact is possible, but never should they be seen as a complete and adequate substitute for that contact.

The eyes I want to gaze into are moist; the hand I want to touch is warm; the crowd by which I want to be surrounded at times of sadness and joy is comprised of people whose names—whose *actual* names—I know. There is a place for the virtual, without any question, and I feel nothing but admiration for those who are expanding and exploring it. But if we are to remain rooted in community, if we are to combat together that "terrible disease of loneliness," that place must to be supplement and not to supplant that which is real. ∎

---

[1] Kurt Vonnegut, *Palm Sunday: An Autobiographical Collage* (New York: Ramjac, 1981), 235. Originally spoken in a commencement address at Hobart and William Smith Colleges on May 26, 1974.

[2] Wendell Berry, "Health is Membership," in *The Art of the Commonplace: The Agrarian Essays* (New York: J. H. Richards, 2002), 146.

[3] See Nate Silver, *The Signal and the Noise: Why So Many Predictions Fail—but Some Don't* (New York: Penguin, 2012), 13.

[4] Henry David Thoreau, *Walden; or Life in the Woods* (1854; New York: Sterling, 2010), 151-52.

Commencement Address 2013

After two decades of formal education and three decades in academia, I have come to the conclusion that there are in fact two canonical texts within which most of life's essential lessons are captured: *Seinfeld* and *The Mary Tyler Moore Show*. This is not to say that either sitcom fully plumbs the murky depths of human experience, but, rather, that if one were dropped from the sky with no knowledge of this peculiar and perplexing world we inhabit, one could do worse than begin with the ruminations of George Costanza, Lou Grant, and their companions.

It was Jerry Seinfeld, for example, who observed that "sometimes the road less traveled is less traveled for a reason," about as good a bit of advice for new college graduates as I have heard in a long time. And then there's Ted Baxter, whose philosophical stylings include the following: "It's actually tomorrow in Tokyo. Do you realize that there are people alive here in Minneapolis who are already dead in Tokyo?"— a conundrum with the philosophical purity of a Zen koan.

By the way, I should note that it is a source of wonderment to me that most of today's graduating seniors were *born* in the year that *Seinfeld* debuted on television and know Mary Tyler Moore, if they know her at all, only as the woman with the botoxed face who appears in infomercials on late night television. This tells me that I am old, and that seems somehow and fundamentally wrong.

The particular passage I want to cite this afternoon is drawn from an exchange between Lou Grant and Ted Baxter just prior to Ted's marriage to the inestimable Georgette. Ted is seeking advice from Lou about how to live happily within a committed relationship. Lou pauses, stumped momentarily by the question, and then begins the following exchange:

Lou: Here's the most important piece of advice I can give you.
Ted: [nods]
Lou: If you're gonna get married, you're gonna have to stop acting the way you do.
Ted: What way?
Lou: The way you *act*. Ted, what I'm trying to say is… you gotta become different.
Ted: Lou…I, I don't think I understand.
Lou: Look, you know how you always are?
Ted: Yeah?
Lou: Don't be that way.

Now trust me, this is profound stuff.

I don't think Lou is telling Ted that he should not be true to himself. (Well, maybe in this case he is, since Ted is a self-centered idiot. But let's assume for the sake of my charge to the graduating class that he is not.) Let's assume that what he is actually saying is that if we are to be successfully engaged in relationships, communities, problem-solving, and meaningful work, we have to possess the ability to step out of ourselves, at least for a time, and see the world in ways that may seem deeply unfamiliar.

It is not always enough merely to "be yourself," which may be among the most overused and misused pieces of advice ever given. Being yourself is relatively easy: you have had lots of practice and it isn't much of an imaginative stretch. Sometimes it is more important to "be," or grasp what it is to be, other people with other perspectives, other beliefs, other ways of apprehending the world. Our greatest moral philosophers and artists and humanitarians have been telling us this for a long time. It is what John Keats meant when he spoke of the poet's gift of "negative capability," that is, the power temporarily to negate the self and experience life through the perspective of another.

It is what Kofi Annan meant when he defined what he called "a citizen of the world in the fullest sense—one whose vision and culture gave him a deep empathy with fellow human beings of every creed and color." And it is certainly what the wonderful novelist Ian McEwan meant when he wrote that "imagining what it is like to be someone other than yourself is at the core of our humanity. It is the essence of compassion, and it is the beginning of morality."

If there is a single trait with which I hope you leave Macalester, if there is a single ability that I hope we have fostered and strengthened, it is the capacity for empathy. With it, you can resolve even passionate disputes; without it you will speak only to yourself and to those who already agree with you. With it, you will be inclined to treat others with respect and compassion; without it, you are liable to become trapped within the echo-chambers of online communities that are anything but truly communal. With it, you can form deep connections; without it, you run the risk of contracting what Kurt Vonnegut called "the terrible disease of loneliness."

It is easy, with all the opportunities you have been afforded, to understand things. It is harder to *be* understanding. And the hard things tend to be the valuable ones. In the spirit of negative capability, I should end by acknowledging that of course there is another perspective on all this—what one might call the *Seinfeld* perspective. It was Jerry Seinfeld who defined the "true spirit of Christmas" as "people being helped by people other than me," and a perplexed George Costanza who asked, "Why would we want to help somebody? That's what nuns and Red Cross workers are for." Your life. Your choice. I know you will make the right one. Just…be yourself. ■

The Liberal Arts College Unbound

From *Remaking College: Innovation and the Liberal Arts College* (Johns Hopkins University Press, 2013)

Demonstrating Value

My opening proposition is relatively straightforward: the continued health and relevance of small, residential liberal arts colleges will be determined by the extent to which such institutions are prepared to focus on quality, distinctiveness, and social purpose. We need to be positioned to demonstrate as concretely as is feasible—and concreteness in these matters can be elusive—that the education we provide has positive outcomes, that it differs in beneficial ways from the education offered in other kinds of institutions (including the virtual), and that it contributes to the collective good.

Together these factors will determine the value of these high-cost, high-impact colleges to students and to the larger society out of which they have grown. Indeed, I would go so far as to say that the commitment to value not only will answer but *should* answer the question of whether these very resource-intensive enterprises, which in the end can accommodate only a small segment of the American population, deserve to remain a prominent part of the higher education landscape.

I believe firmly that the answer is yes, but also that such an answer should neither be automatically assumed nor based on the expectation that nothing about these colleges will change.

Some would argue that the long history, strong reputation, and distinctively positive educational outcomes of the liberal arts college are evidence that change is unnecessary. I would argue, rather, that these things are all in part results of the fact that liberal arts colleges *have* changed in order to remain effective and relevant: rarely quickly and not always obviously to those with too narrow a historical perspective, but change they have. Such change has, in the main, not undermined but has advanced and strengthened their central principles and methodologies, and the coming changes I envision would do the same.

I am regularly surprised by the frequency with which not only the general public, but those of us who spend our careers within the world of the liberal arts college are inclined to view that world as fixed and immutable, ignoring Eugene Lang's observation that "pressures for change have been a historic constant" in the lives of these institutions.[1] The successful liberal arts college, like any healthy organization, must in its nature be organic, adapting and evolving in order to fulfill its mission. Fidelity to an important mission does not mean stubborn adherence to particular means to its fulfillment. Technology and globalization are two of many factors that have in recent years altered what it means to be liberally educated, and colleges that fail to alter their work accordingly will not fulfill their responsibility to their students and to the society those students will serve.

Worth noting is the extent to which both those who predict the extinction of the traditional liberal arts college and those who defend its vitality seem to believe that this issue *matters*. One might argue that such colleges, taken collectively, have already shrunk in relative size to the point where the question of their continued existence is of no great consequence to the future of higher education in America. The percentage of American undergraduates attending liberal arts colleges has declined from about 25 percent in the mid-1950s to about 8 percent in the early 1970s to, by most reckonings, less than 3 percent today.[2] Using the strictest criteria, one might argue that there are barely more than 200 "liberal arts colleges," as traditionally understood, still in existence. Even the most sanguine defenders of these institutions are suggesting neither that this number is likely to grow nor that the cost of the educational methods at these institutions will allow them to provide access to many of the new entrants into American higher education, most of whom are from groups not typically served by high-cost residential colleges. Why spend time either attacking or defending the irrelevant?

The answer, I believe, is that even those who predict the demise of residential liberal arts colleges understand—perhaps on some level just below the conscious—that these institutions have developed an educational model that has been disproportionately successful. According to the National Science Foundation, after normalizing for size, 28 of the top 50 U.S. colleges and universities that produced recipients of PhD degrees in science and engineering from 1997 to 2006 were liberal arts colleges, even though such colleges comprise a tiny fraction of all four-year institutions in the country. By contrast, only 3 of the top 50 were public institutions, one of which, the College of William and Mary, might be described as a public liberal arts college.[3] Richard Arum and Josipa Roska, the authors of the much-cited *Academically Adrift*, which prompted a stream of apocalyptic pronouncements about American higher education, found that students majoring in liberal arts disciplines—identified as areas in the social sciences, humanities, sciences, and mathematics—performed significantly better on a test designed to measure critical thinking, analytical reasoning, problem solving, and writing than did students in other, more vocational and technical fields of study, as did students whose teachers "encourage specific educational practices such as faculty-student contact or engagement in active learning," that is, the practices most common at the small, teaching-oriented college.[4] A recent survey by the consulting firm Hardwick Day found that graduates of selective liberal arts colleges, when compared with graduates of private and public universities, "tended to be more satisfied with their experiences as undergraduates, and more likely to believe that their educations had a significant impact on their personal and professional development."[5]

Clearly, something efficacious is happening at these small institutions that has the potential to inform the practices at institutions very different in kind and scale. Their chief influence is not through size or reach, but through example—an example that will remain powerful only if they continue to demonstrate distinctive success.

Changing Boundaries

One might take this subject in a wide range of directions, touching upon topics from the economic model to the curriculum to admissions policies, but here I would like to focus in particular on the boundaries between the liberal arts college and other organizations and communities. These are in the process of becoming and should become more permeable. This is a positive development, and as this process continues it has the potential to enhance the intrinsic value and the utility of the education we provide to our students.

I would emphasize three main points regarding the boundaries that delimit the residential liberal arts college.

First, as I note above, the distinctions between what is and is not part of the educational work of the college are becoming less clear. Properly managed, this is a good thing. The education we offer our students will be richer and more relevant if we can establish meaningful educational partnerships among colleges and universities and between colleges and universities and other entities, including but not limited to businesses, community groups, non-governmental organizations, and health care providers. We should be able to do more by working together than we can by working alone, offering students not only a larger array of learning opportunities, but programs that are more carefully crafted to prepare them to deal with issues that impact many different sectors of our economy and our communal lives. Without succumbing to the mistaken belief that education is only about vocational training, we should nonetheless be positioned to prepare students more purposefully for local, national, and global workforce needs. And, of course, we should be able to become more efficient in our use of resources. Contrary to what some would argue, there are no easy ways to bend the cost curve in higher education without sacrificing quality,[6] but cooperation and partnerships hold out some hope of productivity gains. We are simply too small individually to do everything comprehensively, economically, and well.

Second, these partnerships and collaborations will only have a deep and lasting impact on our work if they affect the heart of that work, that is, the things that take place in our classrooms, laboratories, and studios. They cannot be add-ons or afterthoughts. They cannot be confined to the realm of the extracurricular, however important that realm is to the development of our students. We do not like to think of ourselves in business terms, even metaphorically, but the fact remains that our core business is made up of interactions between students and faculty and among students in learning environments. We cannot become better at our work if we do not seek relentlessly to improve and advance that core.

Third, we must devote at least as much attention to breaking through and reshaping the boundaries within our institutions as we do to the boundaries between the college and the external world. It is not only the latter that must become more permeable. I am thinking here of internal boundaries of various kinds: those among the departments and disciplines through which we have long organized our curricula; those between faculty and administration; those between what is commonly imagined as academic work and everything else that takes place in a residential community. I not infrequently feel as if these internal boundaries are more stubbornly resistant to alteration than are the real or imaginary ones around the borders of the campus. Every campus in America has a large cohort of those who are, in the words of Ann Kirschner, "fierce guardians of the status quo," [7] and the cohorts may be largest and most determined at those institutions that are the most admired and secure and therefore the least motivated to do things differently. Some small number of institutions can no doubt survive more or less indefinitely in the absence of meaningful evolution, protected by the power of resources and reputation. But no institution, however many applicants for admission it denies, will through this inertia be serving its students as well as they deserve.

An Example of Change

Altering the boundaries around and within the liberal arts college will not in itself lead to the kind of "disruptive" change that Clayton Christensen and others argue has altered other industries and will inevitably alter higher education.[8] While we wait for disruption to come along and put us all out of business, however, such alteration does seem like an important way of adapting to the current needs of our students and of doing a better job of preparing them for the lives they will lead and the work they will do after they graduate.

One example of such change would be the way we at Macalester have responded to the importance and complexity of the set of issues related to global health, which may be the defining challenge of the next several decades and which touches upon nearly every aspect of our individual and collective well-being. Many of our current and future students will make both their living and their mark on the world by working in this area. We should be preparing them as well as we possibly can to do so.

Here is the way a student interested in global health might have pursued that interest at Macalester only five years ago. She might have majored in biology if scientifically inclined or in economics or political science if more interested in matters of public policy. She probably would have found an internship through our Civic Engagement Center with a local organization working on an issue such as reproductive health or the prevention of childhood disease. She almost certainly would have spent a semester studying abroad, probably in one of the less developed parts of the world, and confronted the challenges of global health through both academic and volunteer work. And she might have tied all this together during her senior year in an honors project.

This is a sound and experientially rich educational trajectory that has served students well. What interests me is the question of whether we can do even better by building stronger relationships with organizations outside the college and by rethinking our structures within the college. That is, can we enhance both the quality and the distinctiveness of what a liberal arts college has to offer? In this case, I believe, the answer is yes. Here is the path the same student might follow today.

In addition to pursuing a major, she would add our new academic concentration in Community and Global Health, which brings the disciplines and practices of liberal arts education to bear upon the most important issues related to public health. The concentration crosses traditional disciplinary boundaries, with the core courses alone drawn from biology, anthropology, geography, mathematics, philosophy, psychology, and political science. The curriculum might be described as problem-centered rather than discipline-centered. In addition to its focus on content and theory, the program is designed to develop fundamental skills in areas including critical and quantitative reasoning, writing, and integrative learning. It is (or should be) easier to create such innovative pathways through the curriculum at small colleges than at large universities because our scale allows for more regular social and professional interactions among faculty and, I would contend, because the grip of the disciplines is (or should be) less powerful.

Four years after its approval by the faculty, the Community and Global Health concentration is the most popular interdisciplinary program in the college, with more than 70 students enrolled and steadily increasing demand. We have been able, through a gift, to endow a new professorship in global health that is not restricted to any particular department. Its initial holder will sit in our geography department and focus on medical and health geography.

Similar problem-centered concentrations have been created in Human Rights and Humanitarianism and in International Development. If I were today creating a liberal arts college from scratch, I would move even more aggressively in this curricular direction.

This same student might also be able to benefit from partnerships the college has established with various businesses and healthcare providers in the region, all of whom share an interest in community and global health. Here is one such program:

The Mayo Innovation Scholars Program (MISP) is a collaborative effort between the Mayo Clinic and selected Minnesota private colleges and universities, with financial support from the Medtronic Foundation and Mayo Clinic Office of Intellectual Property, and administrative support from the Minnesota Private College Council. Teams of 4 or 5 undergraduate science and economics majors assist in the assessment of new product submissions by researchers at Mayo Clinic. Each student team is directed by a master's level student and is advised by a Licensing Manager from the Mayo Clinic Office of Intellectual Property. The student teams gain valuable insights and experience in the translational process associated with inventions and product development. The experience culminates with a presentation of the team's research findings, in the form of a business plan, to Mayo Licensing Managers, representatives from the MN Private College Council, the Medtronic Foundation and participating colleges. The presentation is at the Mayo Clinic in Rochester, MN.[9]

Consider for a moment all of the boundaries being crossed in the creation of this program, which has been a stirring success: those between for-profit and nonprofit organizations, between colleges and health-care providers, between what might be imagined as purely academic work and product development, and—maybe most challenging of all—those among various private colleges in Minnesota. Making these boundaries more permeable opens up both a world of educational possibilities for students and the opportunity genuinely to reimagine ourselves.

Roadblocks

Liberal arts colleges, particularly those with relative financial security and reputational strength, should be the cutting-edge laboratories of American higher education. Many of the conditions most favorable to constant innovation are in place: talented and highly motivated students, gifted faculty members, manageable size, close and regular interactions among members of the community, and—maybe most important—a clearly defined mission focused on the education of undergraduates.

I have tried to demonstrate through the example of Macalester College that the evolution that has marked the history of these institutions is ongoing and that change beneficial to students and reflective of the world they will encounter is in fact taking place.

But—and I want to emphasize this point—such evolution is not happening as quickly, broadly, or consistently as it should. I ponder this matter often, and in doing so I try to move beyond oft-repeated jokes about faculty resistance to change [10] and beyond the dysfunctionality narrative that has distorted so much public discussion of higher education among pundits and policy makers. Whether it is in the area of curriculum or collaboration or technology, why do the liberal arts colleges that should be leaders so often fail to lead?

Here is what I do understand: there are virtues to slow, thoughtful, deliberate change and to fidelity to a mission and methodology that have proven effective over time. In many respects, the slow pace of change has served colleges and universities well. Most have survived even as many of the for-profit companies that take pride in their ability to transform themselves quickly have transformed themselves out of existence. Markets create powerful forces, and by many measures the market for those institutions at the high-end of the educational food chain has never been larger or more enthusiastic. Just ask an admissions officer at Harvard. There are precious few examples of enterprises opting for significant change while they enjoy powerful brand strength and an apparently insatiable demand for their services.

And yet, like many others, I cannot escape the sense that economics and technology are combining to create a transformational moment in higher education and that the traditional liberal arts college will be most viable and most valuable if it can use its inherent advantages to make the most of that opportunity for change. I am inclined to set aside the more extreme of the doomsday scenarios for the liberal arts, which, as David W. Breneman and many others have documented, have been around for nearly as long as these colleges themselves.[11] I am even more inclined to dismiss what can only be described as the destructive nonsense coming from those like Peter Thiel and Michael Ellsberg, who argue that a college education itself has become an impediment to financial success.[12] Yet even if liberal arts colleges are not facing a near-term existential threat, they should be actively seeking out those forms of change that will enable them to become better and more productive. The sincere desire to improve may not be as powerful or effective a motivation for change as the fear of extinction—I suspect that most students of the brain would emphasize this point—but it should not be too casually dismissed, and the changes that are born out of aspiration rather than out of fear may in the end be more appropriate and sustainable.

At every gathering of liberal arts college presidents and provosts I attend, at every meeting between administrators and boards of trustees, there is expressed a deep-seated frustration at the inability to move these institutions forward with the agility and creativity the times seem to require. Often these conversations are held *sotto voce*, as if speaking of such frustration, like uttering aloud the name of Voldemort, might bring forth an *Avada Kedavra* curse[13] (which I suppose in the presidential universe is a vote of no confidence). It is that-which-shall-not-be-named.

At the risk of being turned into a toad or an ex-president, let me suggest that the root of the problem lies in our organizational and governance structures. As should by now be evident, I am no fan of the outsized role that the traditional disciplines have come to play in nearly every aspect of the academic life of the liberal arts college. Faculty hiring, faculty evaluation and promotion, the contours of the curriculum, and the allocation of resources are all dominated far too often by disciplinary rather than institutional thinking. It is not at all unusual for a faculty of 150 people to be divided into 20 or 25 semiautonomous units, some of which are further subdivided because of disciplinary tensions —think of critics and creative writers in an English department or physical and cultural anthropologists—or because people simply cannot get along. If it is more difficult to change the direction of a battleship than of a cruiser, it is more difficult still to change the direction of a fleet of small vessels whose captains do not always speak the same language or aspire to reach the same destination.

A version of the same phenomenon has happened within administrations, where we are better at adding divisions and deans than we are at getting them to work collaboratively. This might be expected at mammoth public institutions with multiple schools and an array of different and sometimes incompatible missions. It should not be expected, or at least should be preventable, at a small college.

And then there is shared governance, which can at its best produce broadly embraced, sustainable results but which is all too often not at its best and devolves instead into divided or ineffectual governance. When we speak of shared governance in higher education, we are speaking really of the always complex and often tense interplay between faculties and administrations. Neither group can succeed without the other (though each regularly professes that it would like to give it a try), and no college can reach its full potential if the two are not working effectively together toward at least a general set of mutually embraced goals.

So what goes wrong? In my experience, shared governance works best at the small group level: put a cohort of faculty and administrators together to address a challenging issue and more often than not you will get a pretty good result. These are by and large smart and well-motivated people who are trained to ask critical questions and solve challenging problems. Shared governance also works best when faculty embrace the notion of *representative* governance and trust those they have selected to be their representatives.

Shared governance works worst when decision-making moves from the level of the small group to the level of the whole, which at a liberal arts college typically means the faculty meeting, and when faith in elected representatives goes missing. Faculty meeting votes on critical institutional questions have become to the governance of liberal arts colleges what ballot initiatives have become to the governance of the state of California. Often those who have spent the least time thinking about a strategic process are given the most power to determine its outcome. As with ballot initiatives, that outcome is more often determined by rhetorical flair and political energy than by extended consideration of the common good.

Accountability also matters. I believe that governance is likely to work best when those responsible for decisions know that there is some reasonable chance that they will be held accountable for the impact of those decisions. While the process of administrative accountability in academia is far from perfect, there are at least formal and informal mechanisms in place for removing presidents, provosts, and deans whose decisions consistently have a deleterious impact on an institution, and the relatively short average tenure of those who hold these positions suggests that these mechanisms are not infrequently employed. There is not and should not be a comparable system in place for faculty, creating a separation between decision-making and accountability that is found in few other workplaces and that does not increase the likelihood of good outcomes.

Richard Morrill, President of the Teagle Foundation, has observed that shared governance at colleges and universities is profoundly difficult to revise or even discuss because, for many, it has an ethical as well as an organizational dimension.[14] Challenges to the prevailing governance model are seen as challenges to academic freedom, as administrative power-grabs, or as increasing the likelihood that non-academic influences will unduly shape the curriculum. The best governance models, however, are those that are designed to produce the best results and not those designed chiefly to prevent the worst. While the system in place at most colleges, by passing so much through the blender of relentless campus scrutiny, does a thorough job of smoothing out any impurities, it too often substitutes the broadly palatable for that which is truly original and exciting. One has to balance the ethical imperative that shapes our current governance model against another ethical imperative of perhaps greater weight, that is, the responsibility to serve our students as well as we possibly can.

Because my general preference is for those who are outraged by what I say to be outraged by what I actually say, let me be as clear as I can on this endlessly contentious issue. Good institutional stewardship requires the perspective and understanding that come only through extensive study and thought. Faculty members and administrators who are prepared to devote themselves to this effort should partner in an effective system of shared governance. Administrators who are not so prepared should be replaced; faculty members who are not so prepared should *not* be replaced, but neither should they be the drivers of institutional decision-making. It is unrealistic and unproductive to imagine that all or most members of a faculty will be able to do this work, so a system of representative governance, with a subset of the faculty given the time and responsibility to engage with important strategic questions, stands a better chance of achieving good outcomes than does the system of direct democracy in place at so many small colleges.

The bad news is that these problems are real and pervasive. The good news is that because they are rooted in organization and governance rather than in some intractable antipathy between faculty and administration or within faculties, they are fixable. I would begin by centralizing more decisions that have real potential to impact the direction of an institution and by relying more heavily on representative forms of governance, whether through a committee structure or task forces or a college senate that has genuine rather than nominal decision-making authority. The key distinction, again, is not between faculty and administration, but between those in either group who are prepared to spend time and energy on consequential strategic decisions and those who are not. We should not expect all faculty members, whose central work is teaching and scholarship, to do so; we should also not expect all of them to be well positioned to be stewards of institutional well-being. We might draw some important conclusions from the fact that the one process on most liberal arts college campuses that relies most heavily on representative governance—the reappointment, tenuring and promotion of faculty—is also perhaps the most consequential and the one that on many campuses works most effectively.

I am keenly aware that much of what I am suggesting is more easily imagined than accomplished. To paraphrase Dickens in *Little Dorrit*, when it comes to structural change on college campuses, we are far more adept at determining How Not [or Why Not] to Do It than we are at Doing It. There are of course risks whenever more authority is invested in fewer people, and there are risks—professional and institutional—when one questions a set of governance practices and cultural norms as deeply ingrained as those in academia. But there are risks as well in avoiding change because it is difficult, and these may, for many institutions, ultimately be the greater ones.

In the end, I believe that the future relevance and viability of the liberal arts college may be determined by our ability to create organizations and governance processes that foster more than they inhibit creative change. Fail in this effort and we do indeed risk obsolescence; succeed, and we have the opportunity to offer an education to our students of unparalleled excellence and compelling social value. ■

[1] Eugene M. Lang, "Distinctively American: The Liberal Arts College," in *Distinctively American: The Residential Liberal Arts College*, ed. Steven Koblik and Stephen R. Graubard (New Brunswick: Transaction, 2000), 138.

[2] See Francis Oakley, "The Liberal Arts College: Identity, Variety, Destiny," in *Liberal Arts Colleges in American Higher Education: Challenges and Opportunities*, ACLS Occasional Paper No. 59 (New York: ACLS, 2005), 5. Much of this reduction in percentage, of course, is a result of the proliferation of institutions and the increasing variety of institutional types.

[3] "Baccalaureate Origins of S&E Doctorate Recipients," National Science Foundation InfoBrief, July 2008, 6.

[4] Richard Arum and Josipa Roksa, *Academically Adrift: Limited Learning on College Campuses* (Chicago: U of Chicago, 2011), 109; see also 104-109. The test alluded to is the Collegiate Learning Assessment, or CLA.

[5] Kevin Kiley, "Better Than Yours," *Inside Higher Education*, 16 November 2011. An executive summary of the study can be found at http://collegenews.org/news/2011/liberal-artscollege-graduates-feel-better-prepared-for-lifes-challenges-study-finds.html.

[6] By far the best discussion of this subject is by Robert B. Archibald and David H. Feldman in *Why Does College Cost So Much?* (New York: Oxford, 2010).

[7] Ann Kirschner, "Innovation in Higher Education? HAH!" *The Chronicle Review*, 13 April 2012, B7.

[8] See Clayton M. Christensen and Henry J. Eyring, *The Innovative University: Changing the DNA of Higher Education From the Inside Out* (San Francisco: Jossey-Bass, 2011). I am not wholly convinced that Christensen's template for change can be applied as easily to education as to some other enterprises, but he is worth reading.

[9] http://www.macalester.edu/academics/biology/studentopportunities/mayo/

[10] My favorite offering in this genre comes from Jim Collins, who quotes an unnamed university president as describing tenured faculty as "a thousand points of no." *Good to Great and the Social Sectors* (Boulder, CO: Jim Collins, 2005), 10.

[11] Breneman writes "that when one reads the literature on private colleges one discovers a nearly unbroken history of concern for their survival." "Liberal Arts Colleges: What Price Survival?" in *Higher Learning in America, 1980-2000*, ed. Arthur Levine (Baltimore: Johns Hopkins, 1994), 86.

[12] Peter Thiel is the billionaire, libertarian founder of PayPal who, having received B.A. and J.D. degrees from Stanford, now argues that students should not attend college. His Thiel Foundation pays a small group of gifted students not to do so. Michael Ellsberg is the author of *The Education of Millionaires: It's Not What You Think and It's Not Too Late* (New York: Portfolio, 2011), in which he argues that a college education is a hindrance to entrepreneurial success. His B.A. is from Brown.

[13] Instant death. Unforgivable.

[14] Remarks at meeting of the American Association of Colleges & Universities Presidents' Trust, Washington, D.C., 30 April 2012.

On Civility and Compromise

The State of Civil Society at Macalester

From *Macalester Today*, Winter 2004

Recently I was fortunate enough to attend a lecture by Stephen Carter, Professor of Law at Yale University and among our most powerful writers on topics including religion, race, and ethics. Carter's central point was that the basis of civil society, and especially civil society within a democracy, was a willingness to wrestle with complexities, to argue cogently for one's beliefs, and— maybe most important—to treat those with whom we disagree charitably and with respect. Not surprisingly, Carter notes little evidence of this willingness in the political discourse of the present moment. "We've become extremely good," he observed, "at announcing our positions but terribly bad at defending them." And then, in a remark that possesses the strangely eloquent power of simple truths, he noted that "the reason hard questions are called 'hard questions' is that they are *hard* questions."

Carter's lecture led me to reflect upon the state of civil society at Macalester and, by and large, to be encouraged. Twice in recent months the willingness of this community to wrestle thoughtfully and respectfully with "hard questions" has been tested and, at least in my view, twice we have passed. The first instance was during this year's iteration of the International Roundtable, an annual symposium focused on matters of national and global consequence. Speakers including Niall Ferguson, Tariq Ali, and Michael Ledeen addressed the issue of America and global power from a range of perspectives, some of which are clearly minority viewpoints on the Macalester campus. With a few exceptions—there are always exceptions— we were up to the challenge, and the discourse over three days was intense, provocative, civil, and deeply valuable both substantively and symbolically.

Even more visible has been the ongoing discussion of balancing quality and access at the college, a discussion that for some can be distilled down to the question of whether or not we can and should maintain our current version of "need-blind" admissions. I cannot in this column summarize the substance of this discussion; for that, I refer you to my letter in the last issue of this magazine, the Macalester website, and any number of issues of *The Mac Weekly* published throughout the fall. Here I will simply note that in a variety of settings—an open forum for alumni, an on-campus debate, meetings with student government and the Alumni Board, faculty meetings, informal discussions and emails—the majority of the exchanges have been reasoned and fair, reflective of a community that cares deeply and thinks energetically about hard questions.

One recent graduate wrote in a message to me that, "Macalester alumni react with their hearts but decide with their heads." While I am not sure that heart and head, emotion and reason, can or should be so neatly disentangled, I take him to mean that our alumni are prepared to move beyond pronouncements and to engage with the kinds of nuanced challenges that the broader public, unhappily, too often seems inclined to look past. The evidence suggests that he is correct.

There is, of course, another view: that is, that less thoughtful and more demagogic tactics work, that they "win," and that therefore one should adopt them on behalf of a cause in which one passionately believes. Certainly this assumption appears to dominate the current political landscape on both the national and local levels, and there is some evidence to suggest that it is accurate. My response is merely to observe that each of us must come to an understanding of what constitutes "winning." If prevailing in a battle of ideas means adopting tactics that undermine the nature of civil society, there may be times when it is better to lose.

Near the end of his lecture, Stephen Carter recalled a long-ago conversation with the great Thurgood Marshall, for whom he had clerked nearly a quarter century earlier. Carter had asked Marshall to describe his impressions of John W. Davis, his opponent in *Brown v. Board of Education* and perhaps the foremost litigator of his time. Passing on the opportunity to attack, Marshall instead surprised Carter by volunteering the following observation: "John W. Davis? A good man. A great man. He was just all wrong about that segregation thing." This came from a person who had literally risked his life in the fight for equality and justice and who had every reason in the world to treat his antagonists with the deepest of contempt. If Marshall could demonstrate such humanity and grace, what should the rest of us ask of ourselves, who have been much less sorely tested? ∎

Negotiating the Creative Tensions at Macalester

From *Macalester Today*, Spring 2004

By the time you read this column, I will have been president at Macalester for nearly a year and will have starred in "Meet the President" events in Scottsdale, Tucson, Los Angeles, San Francisco, Naples, Fort Lauderdale, Seattle, London, New York, Boston, Washington, Chicago, and (five times) the Twin Cities. Between these events and Reunion, I will have spoken with, to, and in front of more than 2,000 alumni and parents and will have discovered a number of things: the likelihood of an upgrade as a Frequent Flier on Northwest Airlines (moderate); the most expensive city in which to catch a cab (Boston, hands down); the chance that a package of cookies scrounged in a Northwest World Club will remain intact in a crowded briefcase (small, unfortunately). More usefully, I will have developed a much deeper sense of those issues that are of most importance to the extended Macalester community and a clearer understanding of my mission and challenges as president.

Despite variations in geography and demographics among these numerous events, what has been most striking has been the consistency with which a small set of themes has been articulated by those in attendance—which suggests not only that Mac alumni from different generations have much in common, but also that our collective response to those themes will define the future and shape the nature of the college. Each of these might be described, fittingly enough, as a sort of creative tension, or as a desire to bring into appropriate balance a pair of entwined but competing priorities. I would identify the most consequential of these as follows:

(1) Commitment and criticism: Macalester alumni for the most part care deeply about the college and remain convinced that its central mission is admirable and necessary; at the same time, Macalester alumni—not a few of whom are passionate and idealistic—hold the college to high standards in virtually every sense and are not slow to point out where the college has failed to meet those standards. More than most colleges, I suspect, we are regularly asked, for better or worse, to prove to our alumni that we are living up to their goals and expectations. This perhaps begins to explain why an accomplished and attentive group of alumni has not historically been as supportive of Macalester as one might expect and why it is so critical that we build a sense of trust within our community.

(2) Excellence and distinctiveness: Most of our alumni are pleased with the college's rising national prominence and with our ability to compete for students, resources, and recognition with the finest colleges and universities in the country. At the same time, our alumni are wary of any attempt to "chase rankings" or to become a carbon copy of other elite institutions. We want to be outstanding, but to be so in a way that resonates with the distinctive character, mission, and history of Macalester. In particular, even as we receive more and more applications and become necessarily more "selective," we want to preserve our focus on educating engaged and informed global citizens.

(3) Quality and access: Virtually all our alumni want our programs, faculty, and facilities to be comparable or superior to those at the very finest liberal arts colleges; at the same time, they take great pride in the fact that Macalester serves, and has long served, a population much more diverse economically and much more international than do nearly all of our peer institutions. This commitment represents an enormous investment of resources. Can we devote the necessary funds to the operations of the college while simultaneously providing much more financial aid than do the schools with which we compete for students? Can we foreground access while at the same time ensuring that the college to which we are providing access remains strong and financially stable? These last are perhaps the most pressing questions currently faced by Macalester and will, consequently, be the subject of intensive discussion and planning in the weeks and months ahead.

It should I hope be apparent that none of these "creative tensions" is subject to easy resolution; it might even be fair to say that none is resolvable in the strictest sense, but that the goal should be to maintain the paired objectives in some appropriate balance and not allow one to overwhelm or obliterate the other. On all, to be sure, we invite your reflections and ideas, and on all we will be consultative and forthcoming. Exercising stewardship means not merely celebrating accomplishment or bemoaning weakness, but wrestling day to day, week to week, with issues of consequence and complexity. I hope you will join me in doing so. ■

Commencement Address 2006

During the first two years in which I was called upon to deliver a charge to the graduating class, I managed with not inconsiderable effort to avoid any reference to Charles Dickens, the novelist to whom I devoted the better portion of my once-scholarly life. That streak is about to end.

In Dickens's novel *Little Dorrit*, not one of his better known but in my view one of his best, the tenth chapter begins with the promising title "Containing the Whole Science of Government." The chapter is devoted to a description of the operations of the Circumlocution Office, "which was (as everybody knows without being told) the most important Department under Government." This department was important because it had mastered what Dickens calls "the one sublime principle involving the difficult art of governing a country": that is, "whatever was required to be done, the Circumlocution Office was beforehand with all the public departments in the art of perceiving—HOW NOT TO DO IT."

"Through this delicate perception, through the tact with which it invariably seized upon it, and through the genius with which it always acted on it, the Circumlocution Office had risen to overtop all the public departments; and the public condition had risen to be—what it was.... It is true that How not to do it was the great study and object of all public departments and professional politicians all round the Circumlocution Office. It is true that every new premier and every new government, coming in because they had upheld a certain thing as necessary to be done, were no sooner come in than they applied their utmost faculties to discovering How not to do it. It is true that every [newly elected official]...who had been asking...why it hadn't been done, and who had been asserting that it must be done, and who had been pledging himself that it should be done, began to devise, How it was not to be done....but the Circumlocution Office went beyond [this, it]...went on mechanically, every day, keeping this wonderful, all-sufficient wheel of statesmanship, How not to do it, in motion."

I dwell on these comments because it often seems to me as if college administrations are judged to be practicing with extraordinary facility the art of How not to do it. No matter whether the issue be Cheebadanza or Coca-Cola, study away or global citizenship, financial aid or residential life: we seem, at least to some, to be laboring away in our offices and at our computers, in our committee meetings and our planning groups, with the grand goal of determining in the end How It Should Not Be Done. This is peculiar because I have yet to attend a single meeting at Macalester at which How not to do it was even an agenda item; yet to see a single job description in which How Not To Do It is among the explicit responsibilities; and yet to have a single conversation in which a person boasted of his or her ability not to do it more consistently and effectively than the person across the hall. Maybe most telling, our Office of Human Resources has yet to include not doing it as a criterion for a merit pay increase.

In trying to extract from this conundrum a message for our graduates, I have been able to come up with only the following. Your work will be more productive, your lives more content, and your sleep more restful if you learn sooner rather than later that those issues are very rare on which there is only one instructive perspective. Your interactions with those for whom you work and those who work for you will be more fruitful if you trust that most people—not all certainly, but most—are typically doing their best to carry out in good faith tasks in whose value they believe. Your actions will be more wise and just if you remember that leading often means not choosing between the good and the bad —that would be too easy—but choosing among competing goods, some of which can only be fully realized at the expense of others.

Certainly all this is generally true within the world of colleges and other nonprofit organizations, where no one is getting rich, where board members give rather than get, where the value of the mission is broadly understand, and where the villains— those really trying not to do it—are pretty few and far between.

I know that this may sound to some in our wonderfully passionate and engaged community like a call to compromise principle, so let me be very clear about what I am saying. It is not that all good is relative, all resistance wrong, or all outcomes the result of compromise (though this last is more often than not the truth). It is, rather, that the hard work of change and improvement is more effectively carried out by those with sympathetic imagination and an abiding generosity of spirit than by those whose perspectives are circumscribed by a sense of infallibility and moral certitude. I believe that the most inspiring and successful leaders, the most profound thinkers, and the most gifted artists either learn or instinctively understand this, and I believe that all of us should try within our more limited capacities to follow their example.

It was not Dickens but William Butler Yeats who wrote, in a prayer for his daughter, that "hearts are not had as a gift but hearts are earned/By those that are not entirely beautiful." I will leave you with that observation as a gift, and with my very best wishes for your future success and happiness. ∎

In Defense of Boredom

From *Macalester Today,* Spring 2008

"Boredom flourishes...when you feel safe.
It is a symptom of security." —EUGENE IONESCO

For most people a summons to jury duty has roughly the attractiveness of an invitation to spend a week relaxing in the waiting room of the local Department of Motor Vehicles. Certainly this was my response when I received my own summons recently, and my expectations were, to be honest, borne out by the experience, which consisted chiefly of sitting with over a hundred other souls—sans cell phones, computers, and other electronic forms of work or entertainment—in a sparsely furnished room in the basement of the Ramsey County Courthouse and...waiting.

(As an aside, I should note that I had for company a current Macalester senior, a Macalester alumna, and a member of the Macalester staff, demonstrating clearly that the college is doing its part to keep the wheels of justice grinding.)

Once during the week I was called, together with two dozen of my peers, into an actual courtroom, where each of us was asked more or less the same series of questions, some biographical and some of a more philosophical nature, these last, apparently, designed to identify those lacking all sense of fairness, judgment, or basic human decency. (Not surprisingly, everyone of the panel acknowledged under oath to being fair, discerning, and decent.) After a suitable interval I was apparently deemed a less than ideal juror by the defense attorney or prosecuting attorney or both (or maybe by the judge, for that matter) and dispatched back to the waiting room in the basement to—naturally—wait some more.

My jury service—or, more accurately, my jury availability, since I was never in fact impaneled—happened to take place the week after the Iowa caucuses and during the week of the New Hampshire presidential primaries, which reminded me of another frequently experienced adventure in tedium: waiting in line at the polling place, sometimes for more than an hour and frequently, in Minnesota, in the rain or snow, in order to exercise the right to cast my ballot.

Such moments are often the source of complaint, and I confess to being a regular complainer: my time as a juror-in-waiting, for instance, caused me to miss two important conference calls and to crowd into subsequent weeks all the various meetings, tasks, and appointments that had been necessarily delayed. All this, I am given to complain, in order to do absolutely nothing at excruciating length.

Yet in my more reflective moments I am inclined to recognize that it is precisely the tedium, the sheer and numbing uneventfulness of such activities that underscores the extent to which democratic practices are embedded in American society. My jury service also coincided with ongoing spasms of nascent or failed democratic activity in such countries as Pakistan and Kenya, activity that was proving to be chaotic, divisive, and more than occasionally deadly—but never boring.

There are, in other words, many aspects of participatory democracy that we in the United States are inclined to take for granted because they have become routine, including the functioning of an independent judiciary, the right to trial by a jury of one's peers, and the smooth and civil transition of power from one political party to another. It is when such activities become "exciting," when they begin to shock or to disrupt the quotidian flow of events, that they tend to be most in jeopardy.

And so, hard as it is to accept, we should be grateful that being called to jury service or casting a vote or attending a public hearing is by and large a boring activity. These are boring because their existence and relative commonality are taken for granted, and they are taken for granted because they are so deeply woven into our social and political fabric—into the very way that we imagine ourselves. During the vast majority of times, and in the majority of places in the world today, this has remained far from the case.

Moments of tension and confrontation have surrounded such processes all too frequently; boredom has been far more rare.

The danger of course is that we are liable to confuse the routine with the unimportant. The fact that most of us show up as expected to serve as jurors and stand in line in the rain to cast ballots and accept without violent revolution the results of elections are matters about which we should be deeply proud and fiercely protective. It is within such unremarkable soil that free civil society—a most remarkable thing—establishes its deepest roots. ■

Commencement Address 2009

So, for the rest of your lives, you members of the Macalester Class of 2009 will be able to say that I graduated from college in *that* year: in the year that Lehman Brothers and Merrill Lynch and AIG and the Wall Street culture as we knew it imploded; in the year that Barack Obama was elected President of the United States; in the year that the American automobile industry finally hit a wall, spending beyond our means caught up with us, and the global economy suffered what might well be its worst collapse since the Great Depression; in the year of the swine flu... whatever.

What we don't yet know, and can't yet know, is whether this will in the end turn out to be a turning point or a pause, a precursor to a better future or the beginning of a protracted decline. We don't know whether we will decades from now look back on this as the year in which our behavior as consumers changed permanently and for the better; whether this is the year in which we began seriously to address as a nation the potentially devastating impact of climate change; whether this is the year in which health care and education truly became centerpieces of American public policy. All of this will be known eventually, all of it will be studied and debated by historians, but for now, as we are poised at this moment in May of 2009, we can only hope and surmise.

What we can do even in the near term, however, is derive some lessons from the events of the past several months. There are many of these, though I would like in my brief remarks to you this afternoon to underscore only one. Never forget, and do not fail to learn from, the eruption during the past several months of what the headlines have euphemistically called "populist rage." Never forget the spectacle of Senators from both parties tripping over one another to fan the flames of outrage, or the example of congressional representatives of both parties, many of whom voted for the deregulatory legislation that contributed to our present crisis, willing to abrogate contracts and use the legislative process as an instrument of vengeance. Never forget the moment at which a United States Senator called, only partly in jest, for individuals to commit suicide, or the absence of broad public revulsion at his remarks.

As these events have unfolded, I have waited for more of our elected officials and civic leaders to call for calm intelligence and dispassionate thoughtfulness in the face of challenging circumstances; for more of them to remind us of the dangerous and very, very frightening direction in which "populist rage" has too often led; for more to have the courage to affix a name to the self-destructive forces by which some seem to be guided: the rule of the mob.

We should neither forget what history teaches us about the dark places to which such rule can lead nor be so arrogant as to believe that we are above being led to such places.

Make no mistake: there are those across a range of industries who have committed crimes, and they should be punished; there are many more who have acted out of greed and self-interest, and such motives should be repudiated; there are still more who have been thoughtless and self-deluded, and we should create regulations to ensure that such mistakes can never again exact so steep a price on our nation. But instead of working to correct these mistakes, fix what is broken, and doing all in our power to build a more successful future, we have too often seemed overwhelmed by the desire to affix blame and to spend days and weeks—days and weeks we can ill afford to waste—on angry sideshows while our truly pressing problems go unaddressed.

And so I call upon you as graduates of Macalester College to embody in your lives and work a very different, more thoughtful, more constructive, and more humane approach to our great challenges; to bear in mind the dark caution of the poet William Butler Yeats, who warned of a world in which "the best lack all conviction/while the worst are full of passionate intensity"; and especially to remember the example of Abraham Lincoln, who at the time of this nation's greatest challenge called upon all of us to rely on "the better angels of our nature" and not to succumb to hate and fear.

I am confident that your experience at Macalester has prepared you to do this. And so I am hopeful about a future in which individuals such as yourselves will occupy positions of leadership. ■

Commencement Address 2011

I have spoken often throughout my years at Macalester about my distress at the level of our national public discourse, so it will come as no surprise to many of you that I find in today's American town square relatively few models of Ciceronian eloquence, Cartesian logic, or Lincolnesque compassion for one's fellow human beings. This afternoon I want to return to this topic in a somewhat different way, and through the lens of personal experience. Despite the fact that I love to write and am more or less perpetually convinced that I have something worthwhile to say, I have until recently avoided blogging like the plague. The way I figure it, there are already enough channels through which people can very considerately let me know me that I'm wrong, ill-informed, malicious, or incompetent: email is of course still the channel of choice, but there is also the telephone, the personal meeting, the public forum, and that old stand-by, the anonymous note under the door (low-tech, but effective). Why add another opportunity?

The world of blogs is not my world. It is an alien place where people with elegant *noms de plume* like "hypnotoad53" and "yankeesuck" launch diatribes against the United Nations and Derek Jeter. And yet—when I was invited by the editor of *The Huffington Post* education section to blog for those electronic pages, I was smitten. Arianna Huffington: the woman is on *Real Time with Bill Maher* almost every other week. AOL just paid more than $300 million for *The Huffington Post*, and we know that AOL never gets it wrong. How could I resist?

I did not resist. I blogged: an elegant little piece, I think, on the macroeconomic forces that have contributed to the rapid escalation of college prices. Well-researched, pithy, forceful but not overly defensive. At the very least it would add some useful information to an important discussion. What could be bad?

And then the comments started appearing. And I was reminded why I don't blog.

The first one opened with a deft turn of phrase.

"Hogwash." Who, outside the confines of *Masterpiece Theatre*, actually uses the word *hogwash*? Blog readers, apparently. Mr. Hogwash proceeded to blame the rise in college costs on the lavish spending of the federal government, demanding parents, and avaricious administrators. To which I was tempted to reply, "Balderdash!" And perhaps challenge him to a duel at thirty paces with a brace of pistols. Other comments followed in a similarly jaunty vein. "Mr. Rosenberg, you can't be serious." To give this correspondent the benefit of the doubt, perhaps his was a deliberate and deft allusion to early-period John McEnroe, say, circa 1983? At the time that I wrote the blog I thought I was serious, but who knows? I suppose I could have been joking.

Though this particular comment was filled with colossal factual errors (for example, all private colleges cost almost exactly the same), they were stated in such a...heartfelt...way that one could hardly object.

And so it went: "hilarious" (I don't think this was meant as a compliment), gross misstatements about budgets and student-faculty ratios voiced with absolute certainty, a comparison between American college students and the unemployed youth of the Middle East (trust me). One comment referencing teeth and the working class was just coherent enough to be creepy.

Let's be honest. Who among us would not at least be *tempted* to post a response to some of these pseudonymous pundits? "Dear 'elite (underline) academics (underline) know (underline) nothing (smiley face)': Warm thanks for taking the time to reply to my piece on college costs. You are, unfortunately, an idiot. LOL." Cathartic, true, but well beneath the dignity of a college president. Besides, responding directly to angry commenters on one's blog is generally considered the equivalent of tossing a large piece of red meat into the midst of a pack of voracious predators. They will work themselves into a frenzy tearing it to shreds and come back for more, generally by repeating their earlier misstatements in all caps with many exclamation points. All of this does leave me wondering about the effect of the new virtual universe of bloggers and tweeters and Facebookies (I made up that word because I like it) on our public discourse. One hears a lot about the democratization of culture brought about by new technologies and about the breaking down of longstanding barriers to communication. Fair enough.

But maybe some of those barriers were there for a reason, and maybe not all of them are better off in ruins. Do we seem as a society more informed and productive as a consequence of the explosion of unfettered virtual communication? Are we making wiser decisions? Have you ever taken a *look* at the comments that follow any online opinion piece published even by an outfit as mainstream as CNN?

I admit that I find rather comforting the notion of an editor who will, say, check the accuracy of factual claims before they appear in whatever we want to call the online equivalent of print. These days that sentiment makes me feel rather like Mr. Darcy of *Pride and Prejudice* without the humongous estate.

So my counsel to our graduating seniors is to aspire to a higher standard. Text and tweet and twitter away, but remember what your time at Macalester has taught you about such things as the use of evidence, the virtue of a beautifully turned sentence, and civility in one's interaction with others, whether real or virtual. Aspire to a higher standard, and you might, by example, inspire others to follow. There is of course no going backward, no retreating from the current forms of communication, and certainly no predicting what forms lurk around the corner. So what can come of this desire to present an alternative to the "hogwash" and misinformation and personal attacks that seem to be overwhelming our ability to tune it all out? What, I ask myself as an erstwhile scholar of Victorian literature, would Charles Dickens do?

The answer, alas, is stark and unavoidable. He would, I have no doubt, start a blog. ■

Commencement Address 2012

Good stories get told and told again, and I want to begin my brief remarks this afternoon by sharing with you a good story. It was originally told by Jeff Bezos, the multibillionaire founder of Amazon, at the 2010 commencement ceremony of Princeton University, and then recounted recently in a speech by Bill Bowen, Princeton's former president.

It goes like this. As a child, Bezos spent a great deal of his time in the summer traveling the country in the back of the Gulfstream trailer owned by his beloved grandparents—a pair of Texas cattle ranchers. Being clever, he also spent a great deal of time doing quick mathematical calculations. During one trip, while his grandmother, as was her habit, sat smoking in the passenger seat, he used some information gleaned from an anti-smoking commercial and from his observation of his grandmother, did a bit of mental math, and declared proudly, "Grandma, so far your smoking has taken nine years off your life!" Rather than the expected congratulations on his quantitative adeptness, what he witnessed instead was his grandmother bursting into tears.

The lesson he learned from that moment, the lesson delivered with great gentleness by his grandfather, is one he has tried to carry with him for the rest of his life: cleverness is a gift; kindness is a choice. Each of us should in the end be judged not on the basis of our gifts but on the basis of our choices.

Every one of you graduating from Macalester today is in possession of remarkable gifts. Without those gifts—those talents, abilities, passions—you would not have been admitted to and would not have been successful at this rigorous college. You have also received the additional gift, thanks to your families and to the peerless faculty and staff at Macalester, of an education whose quality and value far transcend what most people in the world, indeed most people in the United States, could ever imagine.

But in the end your lives will be judged less by the nature of these gifts than by the nature of the choices you make about how to use them. The ability to argue effectively is a gift; civility is a choice. The skills, education, and social mobility necessary to acquire wealth are a gift; generosity is a choice. The capacity to formulate clearly one's own thoughts is a gift; the willingness to take seriously the thoughts of those with whom one disagrees is a choice. Self-confidence is a gift; tolerance and humility and selflessness—these are choices.

We at Macalester can say with some confidence that during the past four years we have enhanced your gifts. We have tests and metrics and grades to tell us that this is the case. What we cannot know with equal certainty, but what we devoutly hope, is that we have also increased the likelihood that you will make the right choices, that is, the kinds of choices that will contribute to the bettering of the world we all share. My experience with those who have graduated from this college over many decades tells me that for most of you, we have indeed increased that likelihood. My observation of you during the past four years tells me the same thing.

There are certainly some in these challenging times who would tell you that your only responsibility is to make choices that are in your own best interest. There have always been those ready to make that argument, and their voices tend to be loudest and most influential when people are afraid. Do not follow their counsel. At Macalester we don't respond to fear by retreating to our worst impulses, but by thinking and by working to change for the better those things that are making people afraid. We do not marginalize or demonize those who are most vulnerable or who are different from ourselves; we engage with, empathize with, and when necessary assist them. We do not restrict for any group basic human rights and dignity; we offer up these things, with humility and grace. We do not build walls; we open doors.

This is our history, and this is the great tradition you are about to inherit as alumni. So let me offer you my congratulations on completing successfully your course of study at Macalester and on moving from one great community on campus to another—the community of Macalester graduates—that is more far-flung and less connected on a daily basis but that is also large, impressive, and tied together by and through a commitment to the values of the college.

Be well. Enjoy life. Make good choices. ∎

The Frankenstein's Monster of Social Media

Originally published in *The Huffington Post*, March 29, 2013

"I fear the day that technology will surpass our human interaction. The world will have a generation of idiots."
—*Albert Einstein*

Mary Shelley's *Frankenstein* exposes the dark side of brilliance. Our most original and powerful creations, left unchecked by morality and responsibility, can become enormously destructive. Genius without maturity can lead to disaster. Victor Frankenstein learns to harness some of the most mysterious forces in the universe —he is, as the novel's subtitle suggests, the Modern Prometheus—but he never ponders or learns to control the dangerous implications of his own creativity, and the result is disastrous for him and for those about whom he most cares.

Enthralled by what he *can* do, Frankenstein never pauses to ask what he *should* do.

He would have been at home with Twitter and Pinterest. About *The Drudge Report* I am not so sure, since even mad scientists have to draw the line somewhere.

Social media, I believe, are in danger of becoming the Frankenstein's monster of our historical moment. Brilliant people have created powerful tools that allow us to do things unimagined even a decade ago, yet it is fair to ask whether those tools have done more harm than good and whether they are being wielded with a sense of responsibility. Have we ushered in the start of a new and better age, or have we through our own genius created forces whose destructive power is leaving us diminished and less prepared to make wise decisions?

Certainly, like Shelley's protagonist, we are enthralled, in our case by the stunning capabilities that have arisen in this brave new digital world. We get more information. It comes at us more rapidly. It can be accessed more simply and inexpensively. We can talk to almost anyone about almost anything, and we can find people to agree with or shout at with nearly effortless ease. This is remarkable stuff, and to those who, like me, have been adults for more than a couple of decades, it has seemed to come upon us with a swiftness that is hard to fathom.

But I would contend that our excitement at what we can do has gotten far ahead—dangerously far ahead—of our consideration of what we should do. In an age that is being shaped in so many ways by the creation and evolution of new forms of social media, I have been struck by the infrequency of serious discussion about what we have gained and what we have lost or are in imminent danger of losing. We seem caught up in the creative frenzy of Victor Frankenstein, whose "discovery was so great and overwhelming that all the steps by which I had been progressively led to it were obliterated, and I beheld only the result."

Here are some things that I think our present condition has left diminished. They are important. Whether they are worth sacrificing for the benefits brought by new technologies, and indeed whether such a sacrifice is necessary, are matters about which more of us should be talking.

Privacy.

While there have always been those who were willing to violate the tacit expectation of privacy, I believe that the prevailing assumption prior to the rise of social media was that written communications between individuals about personal matters were "private," by which I mean that they were to be shared only with permission and with discretion. Those who violated that assumption were considered to be, well, *violating* something. The assumption no longer prevails. My experience has been that many of those who are active users of social media assume instead that any written communication can be posted on Facebook or on a blog, unless there is an explicit request not to do so (and sometimes even if there is such a request). This public sharing of person-to-person correspondence is seen by these individuals as wholly appropriate.

Honesty.

Because of the omnipresent possibility that private communications will be made public, those communications have become more circumspect and guarded. Any frank expression of opinion or provision of information that has the potential to cause embarrassment or damage if widely shared is much more likely today than in earlier times to be withheld. I recall being advised when I became a college president to imagine that every conversation I held, even those in private settings, had the potential to be broadcast through a megaphone. Now all of us need to bear in mind that potential.

Civility.

I am not unrealistically nostalgic for an earlier age of universal politeness. Nastiness has always been a prominent part of our public discourse. But it has gotten worse, stoked by the new ability to be, at the same time, anonymous, public, and loud. I dare anyone to read the on-line comments section of any blog or news site that permits anonymous submissions and not come away dispirited by the capacity of human beings to heap verbal abuse upon one another when afforded both a stage from which to declaim and a mask behind which to hide.

Generally I am told that one should not read these comments. But not reading them does not alter the fact of their existence and explosive growth, and dismissing them as unserious underestimates the damage such commentary is doing to our ability to speak seriously with one another. A recent study by Dominique Brossard and Dietram Scheufele of the University of Wisconsin has shown that perusing nasty and *ad hominem* comments actually alters for the worse a reader's understanding of the article at which those comments are directed. Put simply, exposure to this stuff makes us dumber and more polarized.

I would contend that when undesirable things like violations of privacy and anonymous invective reach a point where they are taken for granted, it is time to become concerned.

Truth.

Traditional forms of media are of course imperfect, but typically they have made at least some attempt to obtain verification before reporting something as a matter of fact. Today such attempts seem almost quaint, like decorating a room with antiques. We exist now in an echo-chamber of blogs and Facebook pages where "my friend told me" is a sufficient form of fact-checking and where a demonstrable misstatement of the truth can move from one person's web page to a search engine to a very large audience quite literally in a matter of moments. And once released, as we all know, the genie of misinformation is pretty much impossible to put back in the bottle.

Compromise.

Nate Silver has argued convincingly that many of our predictions have become less accurate as our access to data has increased and that those with conflicting opinions become less rather than more likely to reach agreement when exposed to more of the "facts." Though this may seem counterintuitive, upon reflection it makes perfect sense: confronted with enormous amounts of unfiltered information, we are inclined to choose from the gigantic whole those bits and pieces that confirm rather than challenge our preconceptions. In the Internet universe one can find confirmation for virtually any opinion or belief, no matter how outlandish. Distinctions between the expert and the amateur, between the reflective thinker and the bloviator, are blurred by the sheer volume of material and the difficulty of tracing its origin. It is absolutely no accident that the Internet age is an age of startling political paralysis and partisanship. Our access to information has outpaced, at least for the moment, our ability to process it and to draw upon it to reach agreement on matters of consequence.

Self-examination.

Two of the prerequisites for careful reflection are time and silence. Our age affords us little of either. The consequences of a clumsy statement or an error in judgment are more swift and public than in any previous era. What once might have led to self-scrutiny and moral or intellectual growth now provokes chiefly damage control. We have far less space than ever before within which to be fallible and therefore, I would contend, far fewer opportunities to become better and wiser.

While there is no easy way to change the manner in which social media are currently used, there may be some reason for hope. It is common for both social science and social norms to lag behind the evolution of new technologies, and studies like that of Brossard and Scheufele, along with books like Emily Bazelon's *Sticks and Stones*, a chronicle of bullying that highlights the problematic role of social media, suggest that the science at least is beginning to make some progress. According to the Pew Research Center, the most frequent users of social media sites are adults between the ages of 18 and 29.

This happens to be the demographic by which I am surrounded on a college campus, which is probably why I feel awash in a sea of Facebook protest groups and Change.org petitions, many of whose signatories had not actually heard of Macalester College until they decided to join a protest against its egregious behavior. But 18- to 29-year-olds eventually become 40- to 50- year-olds, and I suspect that it is this initial generation of heavy social media users that will, as it ages and matures, help to establish behavioral norms that are more appropriate.

In the meantime, all that each of us can control is our own behavior, meaning that we can model a more responsible level of discourse and, when necessary, push back against the worst violations of accuracy and decorum. When considering a matter of consequence, I never dismiss the very real possibility that I am wrong. In this instance, the enormous potential of social media to do great things like spread education, effect political change, and bring people around the globe closer together might far outweigh those side-effects about which I am concerned. Yet the history of technological progress should by now have taught us that in the quest for greatness we should never abandon human goodness. We have done so before, to less than beneficial effect.

It is entirely possible that we are living out the creative aspirations of the brilliant Victor Frankenstein and future beneficiaries of the age of social media will "bless [us] as its creator and source." Better this than the alternative: that we are giving birth, in the famous words of Mary Shelley, to a "hideous progeny."

Or maybe I should say #hideous progeny. ■

On Fund-raising
and Finances

Logic, Loans, and Access

From *Macalester Today*, Summer 2008

T he "Education Life" supplement to *The New York Times* of April 20, 2008, includes a cover story on the steps being taken by a small number of extremely wealthy and highly selective colleges and universities to increase the affordability of their institutions. Fifteen colleges and universities, including Harvard, Yale, Stanford, Amherst, and Williams, have eliminated loans from their financial aid packaging, and about 20 more have eliminated loans for students with family incomes below a designated level. A much smaller number—six, it appears—have eliminated all tuition for students with families whose income falls below $60,000 per year, and an even smaller number have capped the amount paid by families with income levels as high as $180,000 per year.

There is no way to construe this increased commitment to financial aid by the wealthiest institutions as a bad thing. Neither, however, should we deceive ourselves into thinking that most colleges and universities have the resources to follow suit or that these changes will noticeably increase access to higher education in America. There are more than 4,000 two- and four-year colleges and universities in the United States; collectively these institutions educate most of the postsecondary students in the country, and collectively they bear as much financial resemblance to Harvard or Amherst as do the St. Paul Saints to the New York Yankees. Educational economist Sandy Baum is quoted in the *Times* article as observing, rightly, that the changes I've described are "not going to make a dent in educational opportunity" in the U.S. Let's face it: the students who might now attend Harvard due to more generous aid policies would not otherwise have failed to attend college but would have attended, say, Brown or Vassar or, perhaps, the University of Minnesota. They are not among the millions of Americans who are unprepared for a wide variety of reasons to attend any college at all.

So, whither Macalester?

Macalester is fortunate in being better-resourced than the vast majority of those 4,000 other colleges and universities. We are not, however, in the same position as the institutions that have eliminated loans, all of which fall into at least one of two and more often two of two categories: these are schools that have very, very high levels of endowment per student and/or relatively low percentages of students who receive need-based aid. According to data in the *Times*, the endowment per student ratio at Princeton in fiscal 2007 was about seven times that at Macalester; at the wealthiest liberal arts colleges such as Pomona, Grinnell, Amherst, and Williams, it was about three times that at Macalester.

Maybe more important, most of these schools enroll student bodies that are considerably more affluent, and therefore require considerably less need-based aid, than does Macalester. In announcing a change to its loan policy, Bowdoin College noted that about 40 percent of its students received financial aid. At Macalester the number is about 70 percent. Next year Colby College will spend about $22.5 million on financial aid *after* the change to its loan policy; Macalester, with a considerably smaller operating budget, will spend about $29.5 million.

So as we continue to evaluate our financial aid policies at the college, we are attempting to bear in mind and balance a number of factors. We continue to meet the full demonstrated need of each incoming student and to do so through packages that include far more dollars in the form of grants than in the form of loans. About 76 percent of the aid we provide comes in the form of outright grants, about 17 percent in the form of loans, and about 7 percent in the form of work-study. The total average indebtedness of Macalester students who borrow is about $18,800 over four years, including loans from all sources—a couple of thousand dollars less than the sticker price of a 2008 Kia Sportage. Given the high percentage of Macalester students receiving need-based aid, it would cost the college about $4.5 million per year to eliminate loans—or more than 5 percent of the *total* operating budget for 2008-09. I am fairly certain that the same could not be said for *any* of the colleges and universities that have eliminated loans.

The more interesting and challenging questions are less financial than practical and philosophical: Is the elimination of loans the best and fairest way to increase economic access to any institution? And has the elimination of loans by a tiny subset of American colleges and universities fostered the belief—deeply mistaken, in my view—that there is something fundamentally and even morally wrong about borrowing for higher education, while we accept without much question the logic of borrowing for a house or car or boat? Does it make sense to eliminate loan expectations based on family income level rather than post-graduate plans, so that, for instance, some economics majors who go to work for investment banks will be loan-free while some history majors who join Teach for America will have loan burdens—based purely on the level of family income when they enrolled in college?

Given the enormous demonstrated return on the investment, I do not believe that there is anything inappropriate about borrowing toward the costs of college, so long as that loan burden is kept within reasonable limits. Neither am I convinced that the elimination of loans is the best way to increase access even to the most elite colleges and universities in the United States. I would be interested in seeing if some of the institutions that have eliminated loans for the relatively small percentage of students on aid, or for the even smaller percentage with family incomes below a designated level, could instead devise plans to increase those percentages substantially. Given the choice between eliminating loans for the 40 percent of students on aid or maintaining loans and providing aid to 70 percent of students, I would be inclined to choose the latter as the greater social and educational good.

This is not to say that we have ruled out eventually altering aspects of our financial aid packaging, including our packaging of loans. It is simply to say that our approach to such changes, and to the broad challenge of balancing quality and access, is to be as thoughtful and as responsible as possible within the limits of our mission and means and not simply to play the game of follow-the-leader. ■

The Story of Macalester

*Excerpted from remarks delivered at the public launch of the
Step Forward Campaign, October 11, 2008*

Tonight I want to tell you a story, though not, I hope, one that will send you off to sleep. It is a story that is surprising and unusual, and in the end, deeply inspiring. It is the story of a college that was founded to be, from the beginning, both broadly inclusive and devoted to the highest standards of intellectual rigor, of one that from its birth, and throughout its life, has remained steadfast in its determination to enhance the quality of mind, strength of character, and depth of commitment of students drawn from every social class and every corner of the world. It is the story of a college that embraced long before it was popular to do so the notion that local, national, and global citizenship were intertwined and essential, and that it was the responsibility of higher education in America to prepare young men and women to be leaders in communities of all kinds and sizes, in all places, and all walks of life. It is the story of a small institution that has struggled, sometimes desperately but always fiercely, to survive and thrive and has steadily and inexorably moved toward higher and higher levels of excellence until it has become, proudly and amazingly, one of the finest and most distinctive colleges in the world. It is the story of Macalester, and many of you in this room have had, and will continue to have, a hand in writing it.

More than once as I pondered my remarks for this evening was I drawn to the famous lament of Hamlet: "The time is out of joint, o cursed spite/ That ever I was born to set it right." The time we are living in does indeed seem to be out of joint, and it is more than fair to ask how feasible it is at this moment of economic turmoil and collective anxiety to move forward with an ambitious campaign to strengthen Macalester and how important it could be to believe in and support a small college whose home seems very distant from the seats of power and commerce in Washington and New York and London and Beijing and whose living alumni number in total less than half the current student population of the University of Minnesota.

To those questions my answers are that it is feasible because we *will* not allow—we *must* not allow—it to be otherwise and that it is important beyond measure. Education, as Jefferson and Franklin knew, is the necessary condition of democracy; education is the single ingredient without which progress and prosperity and civil society are impossible. More important still is education at the highest level of those who will be our leaders in health care and government, business and teaching, science and social service. Most important of all is education at the highest level that also instills an abiding sense of responsibility for one's neighbors, seen and unseen, and a belief that with the gift of such an education comes the obligation to give back in gratitude to all those who have made it possible and in service to all those who will never have such possibilities. The rigorous education of humane and responsible leaders: this is the work of Macalester, and I can think of nothing that is more necessary or that demands more emphatically our help and allegiance— not in spite of these times, but because of these times.

Surely the necessity of this work is what led James Wallace to press forward with what Edwin Kagin called "a bulldog's pertinacity and courage" as he sought against enormous odds to raise funds for the college near the start of the last century and what drove his son DeWitt Wallace to insist that Macalester College "must and will continue to grow in importance and in strength, fulfilling its destiny of...leadership of which my father dreamed." Surely it is what led Charles Turck, faced by the enormity of a world war and by more than a few attacks on the college's mission, to write in 1945 that Macalester "is training students to live in the world of tomorrow and not in the world of yesterday," and is doing so by preparing them to grasp in all its complexity the "vast scope of the world stage" on which they "will live out their lives." It is what led a terminally ill Ted Mitau, in his final speech at Macalester in 1979, to remind us that "the human mind is endowed with the capability to improve the quality of life through social intervention" and that Macalester's role was to educate individuals with such minds and such hearts and with the will to bring them to bear in lives of accomplishment and service. It is what led Kofi Annan, speaking just two years ago on campus, to observe that "We all have the power to make choices. We can choose to be silent and turn away. Or we can step forward and take action. Here at Macalester, you"— we—"have chosen to make a difference."

Please do not think for a second that I am so naïve as to believe that we all agree all the time on how best to carry out the exacting and even audacious task we have taken upon ourselves. We do not, and at times our disagreements have been our weakness; they will not go away, but they must be subsumed beneath our shared passion for the college's mission and purpose, which can be and should be our strength. Neither should you think that I imagine us to be successful all the time or in every instance; for that our work is too ambitious. But I would contend that if we are not failing sometimes, if we are not, to paraphrase Robert Browning, reaching always for that which is just beyond our grasp, we are not trying hard enough or reaching for the most essential things.

I had considered, for a while, asserting in these remarks that the *Step Forward* campaign, our gathering this evening, and the work that lies ahead of us over the next three years are not fundamentally about money. And in a sense, of course, this is profoundly true, since our business ultimately is to build a community of educators and students who can, like Archimedes' lever, move the world. But it would be disingenuous to suggest that this can happen without a substantial investment of resources or to forget that Macalester has for too long been under-resourced relative both to our peers and to the work we hope to carry out. And so while our efforts are about students and our mission is about education and service, the *Step Forward* campaign is, at its heart, about the philanthropy necessary to enable our aspirations to be realized. It is about investing in the future and ensuring that the Macalester of tomorrow lives up to the legacy of the past and the promise of today.

Therefore I can announce with unalloyed happiness and with gratitude beyond measure that we have, during the heretofore "silent" phase of the *Step Forward* campaign, made extraordinary and, for Macalester, unprecedented progress toward the ambitious goal that our campaign chair has already identified. More than two years ago we set the seemingly unreachable goal of raising $26 million toward the construction of the breathtaking building in which we are sitting, one that has already enhanced and will increasingly enhance the sense of community and the state of health and wellness at the college. I stand here this evening to tell you that we have done it—that we have reached that goal and have raised more than $26 million for the Leonard Center. More than a year ago we set the goal of raising $7.5 million for the new home for the Institute for Global Citizenship, so that that structure would become not only the most environmentally responsible building at the college, but the first since the construction of the DeWitt Wallace Library to be fully funded by donations. I stand here this evening to tell you, once again, that we have done it, and that a fully funded, Leadership in Energy and Environmental Design (LEED) Platinum building will open on campus this spring.

We have set other important and ambitious goals for this campaign that we are in the process of realizing with your help, including the first phase of a major—and long overdue—renovation of the Janet Wallace Fine Arts complex; the creation of new endowed professorships to ensure that the excellence of our faculty is sustained into the future; support for study abroad and civic engagement and distinctive academic programs; and strengthening the Annual Fund that is so very critical to the operations of the college. Perhaps most noteworthy of all is the fact that the single largest component of the campaign, larger even than the goal set for any building project, is support for need-based financial aid, to ensure that the accessibility and generosity that have been the cornerstones of Macalester, and from which so many in this room have benefited, remain cornerstones forever. Already in this campaign we have raised more money for need-based financial aid, nearly $24 million, than in all previous Macalester campaigns combined.

In sum, as we move into the public phase of the *Step Forward* campaign, we have raised to date a grand total of $100,394,847 toward our goal of $150 million. Through your help and generosity, and through the help and generosity of the thousands of Macalester alumni and supporters who believe in the necessity of our work, we will reach that goal and ensure that the next chapter in the remarkable story of Macalester is the most successful, compelling, and moving yet written.

Thank you, and—in the words of my great friend and predecessor John B. Davis, who is with us here this evening—all hail Macalester. ■

Through the Looking Glass

From *Macalester Today*, Winter 2009

"If you don't know where you are going, any road will take you there."
—*Lewis Carroll*

S urely it is a sign of the bewildering state in which we find ourselves that as I write this column, two months before its expected date of publication, I can only guess at the extent to which it appropriately addresses its subject. That subject is the impact of a recessionary economy and the turbulent credit and equities markets on the work of Macalester. The rapidity with which events are transpiring has made Monday's prognostications outdated by Wednesday, let alone sufficient for the following weeks and months. We seem to have entered a different world, one in which my Chief Financial Officer has taken to quoting from Lewis Carroll more often than from *The Wall Street Journal*.

That said, it seems important to provide you with some sense of how we expect Macalester to respond to the financial challenges by which all of us are, in one way or another, confronted. Put simply, we will respond with calmness, prudence, caution, and ingenuity: with a commitment to our core mission and purpose but a willingness to think creatively about how we can best carry out that mission under altering circumstances over which we have little control.

Though colleges have typically fared better than many other enterprises during economic downturns, we are far from immune to their effects. All of our sources of revenue—tuition and fees, income from the endowment, and income from fund raising—are highly sensitive to external economic forces. John Nelson, Managing Director of Moody's Investors Service, has said that while "the vast majority of colleges are going to be fine," it is "kind of news…for any of them to be in financial stress." Indeed. We are and should be planning for smaller tuition increases, more pressure on the financial aid budget, a protracted period of weak or even negative returns on our investments, diminished access to credit, and a difficult fund-raising environment. We are and should be looking for opportunities to cut costs by being more efficient, by distinguishing the essential from the desirable, and at times by acknowledging that we cannot do everything and therefore making difficult choices.

It is essential as we work through these decisions that we have a clear sense of the highest priorities of the institution. At the top of the list is preserving and indeed continuing to enhance the strength of our core academic work: We exist to educate; students attend Macalester first and foremost because of the quality of that education; and we must ensure that we are delivering on our promise to provide those students with the knowledge, skills, and motivation to be successful and to make a positive difference in the world.

Other very high priorities include retaining and adequately compensating our faculty and staff, without whom that educational work would be impossible, and continuing to make Macalester affordable to an economically diverse group of students. Losing our best people or weakening our commitment to access might in the short term save us some money, but either action would, in the long term, be harmful *both* to the fiscal health and the national reputation of the college.

With those priorities in mind, we will build budgets that are lean and efficient (we are pretty good at this, having had some practice). Where cuts are necessary, they will come first in areas that have the least impact on our core commitments.

The *Step Forward* campaign will proceed as planned, though of course we will be respectful of the personal situations of our supporters. It will proceed not only because the campaign has to date met with remarkable success, but because the priorities for which we are seeking philanthropic support have become no less important now than they were when the campaign was launched and because the need for help from those in a position to provide it is if anything greater than ever.

The anxieties of the moment have a way of turning all of us into bad historians. Now more than ever, we need to remember that Macalester has survived the Great Depression, many recessions, and two world wars, not to mention a series of internal financial challenges that would have crushed many institutions whose leaders and communities had less fortitude. Let me assure you that the college's goal during this financial crisis is not simply to muddle through. It is to ensure through careful planning and fidelity to our invaluable mission that we continue the process of strengthening both our financial health and our distinctive programs and emerge in five or ten or fifteen years a stronger and better place. This is what Macalester has always done, and those of us charged with stewardship of the college today should expect of ourselves no less. ■

From St. Paul to Seoul

From *Macalester Today*, Spring 2010

The longstanding commitment to having a thoroughly internationalized campus at Macalester has always been a distinctive institutional strength and something of an institutional challenge. The strength, of course, arises from the benefits to every student of being surrounded by classmates of varied backgrounds and cultures; the challenge arises from the commitment of energy and resources necessary to bring to Macalester students from more than 80 countries and every socioeconomic class. This is a challenge we have by and large embraced and overcome.

Similarly, having a very international alumni population offers both benefits and challenges. The benefits accrue to our students—and our reputation—from having well-placed and successful alumni in virtually every part of the globe. The chief challenge is maintaining close contact with an alumni population that is geographically so far removed from our campus in St. Paul. Given the importance of alumni stewardship of the college, this is a challenge we must work to confront. This is why I traveled in January to four cities in East Asia with substantial populations of Macalester alumni and parents and where there are high schools from which we recruit, or would like to recruit, talented students: Tokyo, Hong Kong, Singapore, and Seoul. The visit to each city was highlighted by a gathering of the local Macalester community, and the trip included as well meetings with individual alumni and parents and visits to schools such as the American School in Japan, the Singapore American School, and the United World College in Singapore.

Here are some of the important things I discovered. Alumni and parents in each city I visited feel deeply indebted to Macalester and are fiercely proud of the college's commitment to a global perspective. They would like to feel more closely connected to the college today and are anxious to find ways to support our work and particularly our current and future students. Virtually without exception, the alumni attribute their current success and outlook in large part to their experiences at Macalester with faculty and staff members and fellow students.

Here is the most important thing I discovered—or, maybe more accurately, had reconfirmed. Members of the extended Macalester community feel bound together in ways that cross cultural, religious, and social boundaries. They model in their interactions with one another, and indeed in the quotidian interactions that form their personal and professional lives, the kind of civility, empathy, tolerance, and compassion that seems today in desperately short supply. They are citizens of their communities, their countries, and the globe—and our world would be an infinitely better place if there were more of them.

The trip reaffirmed my belief in the entwined responsibilities inherent in being at Macalester and being part of that broader community of Macalester alumni and parents. Those of us at the college must continue to find ways in the face of a very difficult global economy and a challenging environment for higher education to sustain and improve upon our historic mission. The most powerful evidence of all—not surveys and not data but the lived experience of our many graduates—tells us that we are doing the right thing. How can we do it better? How can we be sure to adapt Macalester's focus on academic excellence, internationalism, diversity, and social responsibility to the world we live in today? These are questions that the faculty and administration of the college should be asking every day.

And upon those who have benefited and continue to benefit from the work of Macalester falls the responsibility to support and steward this special institution. I seldom use this column to make pitches, but I feel utterly unabashed in saying that Macalester is an institution that merits the commitment of time and resources of its alumni. This is true whether one lives in St. Paul or Seoul; it is true whether one graduated in 1959 or 2009. Generations of faculty and staff, trustees and donors, have given of themselves so that we can educate gifted people to live fulfilling lives and make a difference in the world. For this to continue—and it must continue—those people must turn their eyes and hearts back to the college and do all they can to sustain it.

Thank you to those many alumni and parents who took the time to meet with me during my recent travels. Thank you to the much larger group whose support of Macalester makes my job a privilege for which I am infinitely grateful. ■

Why Does College Cost So Much?

Originally published in *The Huffington Post*, March 29, 2011

The question above is the one I get asked most often in my role as president of Macalester College and also happens to be the title and subject of a new book by Robert B. Archibald and David H. Feldman, both professors of economics and public policy at William and Mary. It is a book that should be read by anyone with even a passing interest in the answer and certainly by those policy makers who seem convinced that the answer is simply, "for no good reason."

Rather than looking chiefly at the internal workings of colleges and universities, Archibald and Feldman take a macroeconomic approach and examine whether forces in the larger economy have led during the past three decades to a phenomenon with which every tuition-paying parent (and I happen to be one of those, too) is familiar: college costs have risen and continue to rise at a much faster rate than inflation or the cost-of-living index.

To understand their answer, ask yourself another, perhaps unfamiliar, question: what do colleges and dental offices have in common? (A good opening to a joke, I agree.) The serious answer is that higher education and the provision of dental services share at least three important characteristics that impact cost: both rely heavily on highly educated workers; both rely heavily on close interaction between "providers" and "customers"; and both have been made better, but not *cheaper*, by technology. Not surprisingly, college prices and the cost of dental care have risen at a virtually identical rate, and have followed a virtually identical pattern, over the past half-century. Basically, the costs of both have been driven upward by the rapidly rising cost of hiring educated workers and by the tendency of technology to improve quality but not reduce costs. Root-canals hurt a heck of a lot less than they did 30 years ago, but they are a whole lot more expensive.

So why is there no public outrage at the rise in the cost of dental care, no congressional hearings and threats of price regulation? The answer, I suspect, is that even those least interested in providing funding for higher education recognize on some level that access to that education for large segments of our population is critical to the economic and civic health of our country. Dental care may be very important, especially when you have a toothache, but Thomas Jefferson and Benjamin Franklin never argued that it was essential to the maintenance of a healthy democracy.

So college costs get scrutinized and criticized in a way that dental costs do not. In defense of my industry, however, I would also point out that colleges provide subsidies through financial aid that dental offices do not precisely because we recognize that access to education is a fundamental public good. Among Archibald and Feldman's other findings is that college has actually become *more* rather than less affordable over the past few decades for all but those in the lowest economic strata. This latter point is a major problem that must be addressed through a combination of more thoughtful public policy and stronger commitments to access on the part of colleges and universities, but it should not obscure the fact that aid packages have grown rapidly along with college prices. At Macalester about 70 percent of our students receive need-based financial aid, and our highest yield among our offers of admission is actually among our most needy students.

Colleges can and must be more efficient and productive; colleges can and must make some difficult choices in order to remain affordable. But, ironically, colleges have become so expensive in part because we have demonstrated our economic value through the increased cost of hiring the very people to whom we grant degrees. ∎

Education and the National Debt

Originally published in *The Huffington Post*, April 21, 2011

I get it. The United States, like much of the rest of the world, is peering into an abyss of debt that threatens our quality of life, our security, and our potential for future growth. I am the father of two children and very much want them to inherit a country more prosperous, safe, and economically just than the one we currently inhabit.

I am also no economist, which may or may not be a bad thing in discussions of these matters. Even a quick scan of the economic literature reveals no consensus among economists about the relations among debt, investments, and growth, though it is a pretty sure bet that economists writing for the Heritage Foundation, the Brookings Institute, and the Congressional Budget Office are likely to come to different conclusions. As to forecasting the future? I am a big fan of John Kenneth Galbraith's observation that "the only function of economic forecasting is to make astrology look respectable."

Still, history, evidence, and common sense all suggest pretty strongly that higher, better, and more widespread levels of educational attainment are virtually certain to enhance the quality of both economic and civic life. Is there an example to the contrary, that is, an example of a society that has bettered its condition by *lowering* the level of educational attainment of its population? If there is one, my studies to date have missed it.

Yet as we grapple with the current debt burden at the state and national level, we seem determined to slash investments in the one area, education, that has the greatest potential to drive economic growth and social well-being over the medium– and long-term. States in particular seem to be competing in a sort of perverse Race to the Bottom: we'll see your sharp cuts to K through 12 education and raise you draconian cuts to post-secondary education.

Again, I get it. We have a major debt problem and we can't live beyond our means. But we have seen in recent years, in both the public and private sectors, the woeful results of short-term thinking, and we should be capable even in moments of stress of distinguishing between decisions that clearly do not foster economic growth—such as tax cuts for people like me—and those that do, such as investment in the education of our children. Fear and anger do not as a rule inspire our best thinking, and they are driving at this time far too much of our public discourse and far too many of our policy decisions.

Arthur Rolnick is the former senior vice president and director of research at the Federal Reserve Bank in Minneapolis—hardly a hotbed of radical thought. He has for years made the case that the Return on Investment (ROI) for expenditures on early childhood education is extraordinarily high: according to his research, 16 percent annually, inflation-adjusted. So forget for a moment arguments about social justice. From a purely economic perspective, one can argue that the best place to invest a public or philanthropic dollar is in the early education of an at-risk child. This is not only acting in the public interest, but at a societal level, in pure financial self-interest.

The Return on Investment of expenditures on K through 12 and post-secondary education, while not as high, is unmatched by the ROI in most other areas or by the return on tax cuts for the most affluent. Yet we seem systematically to be undermining our public education system at every level. Our flagship public university systems, arguably one of the greatest achievements of American democratic society in the 19th century and unequalled anywhere else in the world, are being devastated. What does it say about our shift in priorities when universities founded during the cataclysmic stress of the Civil War are being dismantled at a time when, despite our challenges, we remain by many measures the most prosperous country on earth?

I am the president of a highly selective private college that is actually benefiting from the defunding of public higher education. As more and more families question the value proposition of once-stellar public institutions, we are seeing a surge in applicants whom we are unable, as a small college, to accommodate. Many of these are students from working-class families who are attracted to Macalester College by our policy of meeting the full need of every student we admit; some are students from families of means who are concerned about larger classes, fewer faculty members, and declining graduation rates at the publics. But I am a citizen and a father even before I am a college president, and I would trade the increase in applications to my institution for more thoughtful and informed public policy at the state and federal level and for a robust system of public education from early childhood through graduate school.

Macalester is a great and respected institution and will thrive. I want to be able to say the same, with an equal level of confidence, about every level of American education and, by extension, American civic life. ■

Hard Times for These Times

Originally published in *The Huffington Post*, May 19, 2011

Prior to becoming an academic administrator I was for nearly two decades a teacher and student of Victorian literature, and in particular of the novels of Charles Dickens. This revelation typically brings responses ranging from mild surprise—how...quaint—to outright shock, as if I were a physician confessing to having done a residency in medieval barbering.

In truth, it took me a long time to understand fully the relevancy of my "residency" in Dickens to the work and the world I now encounter. I can be slow about these things. But I have come finally to recognize that nearly everything I needed to know about my current situation was revealed in Dickens had I only taken the trouble to look.

Consider for instance the influential report on the future of American higher education prepared in 2007 under the direction of then Secretary of Education Margaret Spellings. The report opens with a statement on "The Value of Higher Education" which speaks about "intellectual capital" and "the new knowledge-driven economy" and "economic benefits" and, really, about little else.

Surely the report would have brought a smile to the face of Thomas Gradgrind, the forward-thinking educator in Dickens's *Hard Times*, who insisted that "In this life, we want nothing but Facts, sir; nothing but Facts!" Later, of course, a chastened Gradgrind acknowledges that, "Some persons hold…that there is a wisdom of the Head, and that there is a wisdom of the Heart. I have not supposed so; but…I mistrust myself now. I have supposed the Head to be all-sufficient. It may not be all-sufficient." But I assume the Spellings Commission never got past the first few chapters of the novel.

When I think about more recent efforts by the federal government to regulate and standardize higher education, I recall, from *Little Dorrit*, Dickens's prescient description of the Circumlocution Office, the "most important Department under Government," whose great accomplishment is to be foremost among all government departments in practicing the great art of "HOW NOT TO DO IT." "It is true," Dickens concedes, "that every new premier and every new government, coming in because they had upheld a certain thing as necessary to be done, were no sooner come in than they applied their utmost faculties to discovering How not to do it." But the Circumlocution Office sets a standard to which other offices of government can only aspire.

The financial wizards who have done such good for the global economy would have found a worthy model in Mr. Merdle, also from *Little Dorrit*, a titan of the banking world who is "the recipient of more acknowledgment within some ten or fifteen years...than had been bestowed in England upon all the peaceful public benefactors, and upon all the leaders of all the Arts and Sciences, with all their works to testify for them, during two centuries at least." Ultimately, when it is revealed that Mr. Merdle is in fact "the greatest Forger and the greatest Thief that ever cheated the gallows," the economy of England nearly falls crashing into ruins. But for the first 600 pages things are looking really good for Merdle and his investors.

Our ongoing, systematic disinvestment in the education of our young? Recall the scene in *A Christmas Carol* in which the Ghost of Christmas Present reveals to Scrooge two prostrate, shriveled, and degraded children. "This boy," he explains, "is Ignorance. This girl is Want. Beware them both, and of all their degree, but most of all beware this boy, for on his brow I see that is written which is Doom, unless the writing be erased."

And what of the way we are, during these particular Hard Times, treating those among us who are most vulnerable, most in pain, and most in need of kindness and care?

"Are there no prisons? Are there no workhouses?" ∎

Mr. Bennett and Mr. Bumble

Originally published in *The Huffington Post*, March 26, 2012

One of my favorite moments in Dickens's fiction comes early in *Oliver Twist*, when a young and vulnerable Oliver is brought before the members of the board of the workhouse—some "very sage, deep, philosophical men" who discern "what ordinary folks would never have discovered" about the institution they oversee: "the poor people liked it!…It was a regular place of public entertainment for the poorer classes; a tavern where there was nothing to pay;…a brick and mortar elysium, where it was all play and no work. 'Oho!' said the board, looking very knowing; 'we are the fellows to set this to rights; we'll stop it all, in no time."

So the board sets out with great energy and enthusiasm to make it much less fun to be poor, on the theory that the poor will then elect to be…something else.

Which brings me to William Bennett.

Mr. Bennett is nothing if not consistent. Twenty-five years ago he articulated what has come to be termed the Bennett Hypothesis: the proposition that the cost of college was rising because needy students were being given *too much money* by the government and that if the spigot were shut off, colleges and universities would be forced to behave responsibly and lower costs. Now he is making the same argument again (cnn.com/2012/03/22/opinion/bennett-college-costs). Think of it as his silver anniversary gift to the world of higher education.

The current version of Mr. Bennett's argument would provide Dickens with enough material to compose another novel. He writes that "While increased federal aid does not cause college price inflation, it can be a considerable factor," without ever explaining how or why and while acknowledging that "many other elements influence tuition prices." He cites a 2008 report from the College Board, "Trends in Student Aid," noting with disapproval that "total student aid increased by about 84 percent in inflation-adjusted dollars over the decade from 1997-98 to 2007-08." "Skyrocketed" is his descriptor of choice. He does not however add the following from the same report: the number of recipients of Pell Grants during that period increased from 3.7 million to 5.4 million due to increased college enrollments, thereby actually "diluting the value of these grants to individual students." In other words, aid increased in large part because there were more students, and more students with financial need, attending college. Elysium indeed.

Here is the change in the Pell Grant, in constant dollars, over the past three decades. Maximum grant in 1979-80: $5,368. Maximum grant in 2011-12: $5,550. During most of that period the maximum grant was in constant dollars well below the figure from 1979-80.

In fact, over the past 10 years, and 20 years, and 30 years, state and federal dollars have declined as a percentage of revenues at both public and private colleges and universities. If the government is contributing to the rise of college costs for individual students, it is by steadily and systematically disinvesting in higher education, not by over-investing. In my own state of Minnesota, the share of the state's general fund that supported higher education in 1987, when the Bennett Hypothesis was born, was just under 16 percent. Today it is just over 8 percent.

If The Hypothesis were correct, one would expect to have seen this decline in public support lead to a slowing of the rate of tuition increases. If Common Sense were correct, one would expect to see the decline in state support passed along to students in the form of higher prices. I will leave it to the reader to guess which scenario has unfolded.

The inspiration for Mr. Bennett's reassertion of his claim seems to be the recent publication by the Center for College Affordability and Productivity of a study by economist Andrew Gillen entitled "Introducing the Bennett Hypothesis 2.0." Personally I was prepared to consider version 1.0 sufficient. The director of the Center is Richard Vedder, who is pretty much to government spending what Grover Norquist is to taxes and who has remarked that "there is no doubt in my mind today that governmental subsidies to higher education are excessive–our nation would be better off if we spent less. Indeed, I suspect no governmental spending commitment at all would be preferable to the situation today."

Take note: Our nation would be better off if the government spent nothing on higher education. Here I recommend that you pause for a moment to consider the various implications for our collective future of this particular modest proposal.

Unsurprisingly, Professor Gillen's study concludes that government spending on higher education leads to outcomes that are, in his words, "depressing" and "terrifying." Even he cannot avoid acknowledging, however, that his research suggests that "aid targeted to low-income students (such as the Pell grant and subsidized Stafford loans)...will...be more likely to succeed in making college more affordable and therefore accessible (for low-income students)" than aid that is not need-based, such as a tax credit. But this point is glossed over rather quickly on the way to "depressing" and "terrifying" and is skipped altogether by Mr. Bennett.

College costs too much and this is a major problem, not only for the most economically disadvantaged but also for those in the middle class who neither qualify for many need-based programs nor can afford the full sticker price. Colleges and universities bear much of the responsibility for this state of affairs because they have been slow to embrace creative change and reluctant to make difficult choices. Public disinvestment has played a major role. So too has the evolution of the labor market over the past several decades, which has seen the cost of hiring educated workers rise at a rate well beyond the rate of inflation.

In short, this is a complicated problem whose solution will take careful thought and better cooperation among higher education, the government, and the private sector. But this much is undoubtedly true: while we cannot easily say what the solution to rising college costs is, we can say what it is not. It is *not* reducing support through grants and low-interest loans for those who are most in need. The economic and social cost of not educating these students far exceeds the cost of making education more accessible.

Oliver Twist's most iconic moment occurs when the starving protagonist offers his empty bowl to the workhouse cook and declares, "Please, sir, I want some more." This audacity provokes enormous consternation among members of the staff and the Board and especially within Mr. Bumble the Beadle, who responds to Oliver's request by placing him on more or less a starvation diet—for his own good. This leads Oliver, of course, into a life of poverty, crime, and abuse, from which he is only rescued, in classic Dickensian fashion, by the miraculous intervention of a wealthy benefactor (from the private sector).

My guess is that those high-need students most affected by the economic and educational starvation diet favored by Mr. Bennett, Mr. Vedder, and the Center for College Affordability and Productivity would not in the main be so fortunate. ∎

Educating Minnesota

From *Macalester Today*, Fall 2012

Imagine a state that has for decades been one of the most highly educated and economically stable in the country: where nearly two-thirds of the population has some college education and more than 10 percent of the population is in possession of an advanced degree. According to the 2010 census, this state has the third-best high school graduation rate in the United States, and its students are on average among the best-performing on math and science exams. Not surprisingly, it is home to one of the highest concentrations of Fortune 500 headquarters in the country, and its unemployment rate stood at the end of May 2012 at 5.6 percent, far below the national rate of 8.2 percent.

Now imagine a state that has one of the largest race-based

achievement gaps in the country—where, in effect, students born into affluence and students born into poverty, and students of color and Caucasian students, attend different school systems. Since the year 2000, this state has seen in real dollars a 35 percent decline in per-student support for higher education, as compared to a national decline of about 20 percent. One result of this decline is that the debt burden of its college students is among the very highest in the country. Of its students currently entering college, fewer than half will graduate. Its projected population growth is chiefly among those groups that are least well served by the education system at every level.

Both states are Minnesota.

The first paragraph might be said to describe a standard of economic and civic life that exists today as a consequence of decisions made in the past. The second might be said to foreshadow a much less thriving future that might arise from decisions being made—or not being made—right now.

One of the characteristics of Minnesota that I have come to admire over the past decade is the willingness of individuals and groups to work together to contribute to the common good. It is not surprising, therefore, that there exists in the state an organization like the Itasca Project, a group of leaders from business, politics, education, and the nonprofit world who have formed a "civic alliance drawn together by an interest in new and better ways to address Minneapolis/St. Paul regional issues that impact our economic competitiveness and quality of life." Nor is it surprising that the group has identified higher education as a top regional priority.

For the past year I have been part of an Itasca task force on higher education whose report, *Higher Education Partnerships for Prosperity*, has recently been published and can be found at www.theitascaproject.com/priorities.html.

A couple of things in particular have been striking about this effort. One has been the willingness of individuals from both the business and education sectors—including the leaders of some of the state's largest employers—to devote significant time to understanding and imagining solutions to the educational challenges we face. Another has been the willingness of educational leaders from the public and private sectors—Eric Kaler, the President of the University of Minnesota, and Steven Rosenstone, the Chancellor of the Minnesota State Colleges and University System, both joined me as part of the group—to put aside competition and to think about a cooperative model that would best serve the citizens of the state. I am pretty sure that neither of these things would be possible at the moment in many other places.

Unsurprisingly, the Itasca report does not suggest that there are easy solutions to what might reasonably be termed a crisis in higher education in the state, particularly during a time of enormous economic stress. But a prerequisite for solving any problem is first to recognize its existence, and the report both does that and identifies four specific areas in which the state can and should make progress:

- *Align academic offerings with workforce needs*
- *Foster an ecosystem of research and innovation*
- *Form new collaborations across higher education to optimize system-wide intellectual assets and efficiency*
- *Graduate more students*

Each of these areas will require thoughtful treatment. "Workforce needs," for instance, do include specific areas of knowledge and vocational skills, but they also, and perhaps most centrally, include the graduation of students with the ability to do things like think creatively, write and speak clearly, work collaboratively, and adapt to change. As it happens, we at Macalester think that a high-quality liberal arts education does a remarkably good job of inculcating such abilities.

Anyone who lives in or has connections to Minnesota should care about the work of the Itasca task force. And so, I would argue, should everyone else, since Minnesota's challenges in this area are a microcosm of the nation's. Perhaps the solutions at which we arrive, through cooperation and careful attention to matters of importance, can be a model for the nation as well. ■

On Taking
a Stand

Understanding the Liberal in Liberal Arts

From *Macalester Today,* Summer 2005

N early every issue of *Macalester Today* published during the past two years has included at least one letter or article devoted to the preponderance of liberal viewpoints at the college. Jay Cline '92 observed last fall—with a bit of facetiousness and more than a bit of good spirit—that "there's been an average of 3.7 openly conservative students and 14 closeted right-wingers on campus since 1967." Neither Cherie Riesenberg '72 nor Joe Schultz '06 would disagree, the former expressing concern about "the lack of political diversity and tolerance" on campus and the latter lamenting that "being a Republican at Macalester is a true challenge indeed." A series of letters and columns addressing this topic was published this spring in *The Mac Weekly,* with students alternately bemoaning and celebrating the left-wing perspectives of their classmates.

It would be disingenuous to pretend that these writers have not identified both a reality and a challenge at the college. Our surveys of incoming students confirm what even a casual exposure to campus culture would suggest: most Macalester first-years self-identify as politically and socially liberal. A recent study of college faculties conducted by political scientists at George Mason University, Smith College, and the University of Toronto, moreover, found that "Seventy-two percent of those teaching at American universities and colleges are liberal and 15 percent are conservative," a disparity that reaches across colleges of virtually every sort and that increases at what the authors of the study describe as "top tier" schools.[1] No surprise that Macalester is in many respects a thoroughly liberal place.

Having said this, I believe that it is critical to establish some important and relevant distinctions: between passion and intolerance, between personal and professional responsibilities, and between the views held by individuals within our community and positions espoused by the college of which all of those individuals are a part. We do a disservice to a remarkably thoughtful and humane student body if we assume that the depth of commitment to particular causes and concerns precludes respect for others or the willingness to wrestle with complexities. I would submit that the differences in perspective between Macalester students and Macalester alumni, along with the success of our graduates in a broad range of fields and endeavors, are at least partially attributable to our ability to inculcate the virtues of listening and learning.

I also believe that our faculty are by and large adept at maintaining the distinction between their views and responsibilities as citizens and their charge as educators. No group is perfect, and no one should pretend that the maintenance of this distinction is easy, but anyone who takes the time to examine the work done by our students in political science or economics, history or literature, international or American studies, would conclude that what takes place in Macalester classrooms is not indoctrination but instruction of the most rigorous and professional kind.

The most important (and controversial) distinction of all, in my view, is between the views held and causes championed by individual Macalester students, alumni, faculty, and staff and the advocacy practiced, or not practiced, by Macalester College. No small number of alumni—and a few students—complain that the actions of the college reflect a liberal bias. No small number of students—and a few alumni—complain that the actions of the college reflect an insufficient commitment to a progressive political and social agenda. While it would be overly optimistic to argue that this points to an institution in equipoise, I would contend that such complaints from both right and left are probably inevitable if the college is being responsible in fulfilling its educational mission. Bill Bowen, former president of Princeton University, current president of the Andrew W. Mellon Foundation, and a passionate advocate for access and equity in education, declared in a recent speech that "The university should be the home of the critic, welcoming and respectful of every point of view; it cannot serve this critically important function if it becomes the critic itself, coming down on one side or another of controversial issues, or if its integrity is compromised when official neutrality succumbs to unofficial complicity....It is the freedom of the *individual* to think and to speak out that is of paramount importance, and safeguarding this freedom requires that the institution itself avoid becoming politicized." [2]

Certainly it is incumbent upon us as institutional citizens of local, national, and global communities to act responsibly toward the environment, to respect human rights and human dignity, and to speak out against policies that endanger our invaluable societal function. To help us determine when and how to act on such matters, we have established a Social Responsibility Committee comprised of students, faculty, staff, and trustees. But on issues about which reasonable and thoughtful people disagree, we must be cautious indeed not to preempt discussion or silence dissent by declaring through our actions that some perspectives are right and others wrong. Thoughtful advocates and energetic leaders are best produced by a college that resists the sometimes powerful temptation to engage in advocacy itself and that openly promotes civility of discourse and the frank exchange of ideas. To me, this is the deepest meaning of the "liberal" arts: education as preparation for the challenges and responsibilities of personal, political, and intellectual freedom. ■

[1] Howard Kurtz, "College Faculties a Most Liberal Lot, Study Finds," *Washington Post,* March 29, 2005.
[2] Thomas Jefferson Lecture delivered at the University of Virginia, April 6, 2004

Let's Hear It for Students Who Care about Citizenship

From *Macalester Today,* Summer 2006

College presidents have in recent years become adept practitioners of what Muhammad Ali, following his upset victory over George Foreman, termed the "rope-a-dope" maneuver, which works more or less as follows: cover up, allow your opponent to batter you relentlessly, and hope in the end that he wears himself out. While painful, this strategy is often more effective and certainly less time-consuming than responding to each of the left-jabs and uppercuts directed at our chins.

That said, I do feel the need to offer some response to Katherine Kersten's recent column on the Coca-Cola ferment at Macalester. My aim is not to weigh in one way or another on the merits of Coke's corporate practices or to declare what I will do in response to the recommendation from Macalester's Social Responsibility Committee that we suspend the sale of Coke products on campus. It is, however, to offer a somewhat different perspective than Ms. Kersten's on the nature of our students and the virtues of debate on a college campus.

Two points are worth emphasizing. One is that the perspectives on issues of this kind at Macalester are diverse and varied and that this is a *good* thing. In Ms. Kersten's own column, a Macalester faculty member is quoted as opposing a ban on Coke, and in the *Star Tribune* of April 2, 2006, a letter from a young alumnus appears that also argues against such a ban. In my judgment, a civil and thoughtful exchange of views on complex issues is precisely what we want on college campuses because it is precisely the intellectual environment in which students learn best. The fact that members of the Macalester community engage in spirited debate on such topics is a sign that we are doing our job.

The second point I would like to make is about the "activist" students who, Ms. Kersten suggests, are chiefly interested in "striking self-righteous poses, parading in front of cameras and playing the rebel." Now, I am about the last person who might be expected to champion student activists, given that—as the embodiment of "authority" at Macalester—I am more often than not the target of their activism. But champion them I will. It is unfair to those students to characterize their activities as thoughtless or self-serving. They are indeed young, they are indeed passionate, and they may on occasion be wrong (unlike we older folks who are, of course, more or less always right). One thing they are not, however, is insincere.

I know many of the activist students at Macalester, and I know that when they are not lobbying for particular causes they are participating in hurricane relief trips to the Gulf Coast, doing volunteer work with local community organizations, studying history, philosophy, and political science, and otherwise taking seriously Macalester's stated belief in the importance of service and in education as enhancing the public good. Their sense of what constitutes the public good may not always be universally embraced, but their energy, goodwill, and seriousness of purpose should not be underestimated. I would rather have students who *care* about citizenship, even ones with whom I sometimes disagree, than students more indifferent or narrowly self-interested.

Thomas Friedman spoke at Macalester recently, and, in response to a challenging question about one of his views, observed, "You can call me *wrong*, but you can't call me naïve." About our passionate students I would insist upon something similar. It is fair enough to contend that they are incompletely informed or even flat-out wrong; it is less fair to contend that they are motivated by anything other than a desire to serve the communities whose leaders they will, one day, become. ■

Land of Dreams or Darkling Plain? Macalester and Environmental Responsibility

From *Macalester Today,* Summer 2007

Matthew Arnold's poem "Dover Beach," written around 1851 though not published until 1867, is often seen as helping to usher in the distinctive melancholy and looming apprehension of what has come to be called the modern age. The poem begins peacefully enough—"The sea is calm tonight./The tide is full, the moon lies fair/Upon the straits"—but soon exposes the anxiety and dangers lurking just beneath the superficial tranquility of the landscape:

> *...for the world, which seems*
> *To lie before us like a land of dreams,*

So various, so beautiful, so new,
Hath really neither joy, nor love, nor light,
Nor certitude, nor peace, nor help for pain....

Arnold seems unhappily prescient in foreseeing the despair, conflicts, and deadly challenges of the ensuing century and a half. And nowhere does he seem more accurately predictive than in his anticipation of the literal and growing threats to the seemingly eternal loveliness of the natural environment. Indeed, of all the ways we have proven ourselves capable of wreaking havoc on the planet and on one another, none may in the end turn out to be more devastating than our ongoing disruption of the longstanding balance of the airs, seas, and land. Our environmental mistakes and the urgent need to address them will almost certainly be the preeminent challenge to humanity in the 21st century.

For this reason I believe that colleges and universities cannot remain neutral on the issue of environmental responsibility. As I have said and written many times before, colleges must typically avoid the temptation to stake out positions on controversial issues so that they can remain places within which conflicting views can be carefully developed and freely expressed. I also believe, however, that we are long past the period of reasonable disagreement about the need for higher levels of environmental stewardship.

At Macalester we are taking a number of steps to make real and concrete our commitment to this critical aspect of responsible global citizenship. We have signed on as members of the Leadership Circle of the American College and University Presidents Climate Commitment, an effort that will lead the college to take a variety of steps to reduce in the near term our emission of greenhouse gases and to achieve in the long term the goal of climate neutrality. This goal will over time affect the products we purchase, the staff positions we create, the behavior we encourage, and the spaces we build.

On that last subject, it is important to note the steps we have taken and will take as we continue the perpetual process of renewing the campus infrastructure. The new Macalester Athletic and Recreation Center was thoroughly redesigned to reduce its energy usage, and the old building was not demolished but deconstructed so that 90 to 95 percent of its materials can be reused or recycled. The renovation and expansion of the Janet Wallace Fine Arts Complex will be similarly attentive to sustainability. And in building the new home for the Institute for Global Citizenship at the corner of Grand and Snelling Avenues, we have set as our goal the achievement of LEED Platinum certification for the building. LEED, or Leadership in Energy and Environmental Design, is the most widely accepted green building rating system in the world. Only a handful of buildings worldwide have received a platinum rating, the highest possible, and to date only one building in Minnesota has even applied for a rating at that level.

Most significant of all have been the many student-led environmental initiatives that have begun to alter the way we think and behave as a community. This week I will be joined by St. Paul Mayor Chris Coleman at the dedication of the college's second student-led green roof project, this one atop Kagin Commons. Macalester students have inspired the development of a Clean Energy Revolving Fund (CERF) that will help fund future projects focused on sustainability and act as a viable financial model for other institutions. Indeed, a pamphlet by Macalester sophomores Asa Diebolt and Timothy Den Herder-Thomas, entitled *Creating a Campus Sustainability Revolving Loan Fund: A Guide for Students*, has been published by the Association for the Advancement of Sustainability in Higher Education (www. aashe.org/highlights/cerf.php). Student membership in the Macalester Conservation and Renewable Energy Society (Mac-CARES) is growing, and the activity is rigorous and intense.

It would be misleading to pretend that all of the steps we might take to transform the campus into a more energy-efficient and environmentally responsible place will be easy or quick or that we have reached consensus on how to proceed: the costs and trade-offs will in some cases be painful and very difficult in the near term; the alterations in expectations and habits will in some cases be slow. But I fear that failure will leave us collectively in the position of the anguished and bereft speaker at the conclusion of "Dover Beach":

> *And we are here as on a darkling plain*
> *Swept with confused alarms of struggle and flight,*
> *Where ignorant armies clash by night.* ■

What Am I Doing Here?

Macalester Convocation Address, September 2009

G ood afternoon, and welcome to the opening convocation of the 2009-10 academic year, recessionary version 2.0. In some years, I am forced to confess, we write a hefty check to an outside speaker who proceeds to tell you what you already knew, cared little about, or thought you cared about until you sat through the speech. This year, given the tightness of money all around, my staff decided that I was the perfect person to do such a thing for free. And so here we are. I will do my best not to disappoint.

Each spring I have the privilege of hosting at my home a group of students who have been honored with what we call the Presidential Leadership Award. These are graduating seniors who have demonstrated in their academic, co-curricular, and service work the qualities of leadership especially valued at Macalester. Often these are students I have come to know pretty well, so I was struck last April when not one but two of them asked me exactly the same question: what is it that you do, anyway? The question was asked not as a challenge but out of a genuine sense of curiosity. They knew that, being the president, I must do *something*, and that given the size of my office and my residence in a college-owned house, it must be something reasonably important. They knew that if they were in my general vicinity they were likely to get their picture taken; that I served as a kind of collegiate maitre d', welcoming everyone from new students to visiting dignitaries to campus; and that my name appeared in *The Mac Weekly* more often than most, particularly on the opinions page. But whereas they could define pretty precisely the jobs of their professors and their coaches and their residence hall directors, they could not define mine.

So I thought I would use this opportunity to offer a few observations about my job: not by taking you through a typical day or week, which would constitute a less than exhilarating address, but by talking a bit about the responsibilities that college presidents do or do not, or should or should not, take on. At the very least it may mean that I get asked a little less often what I'm doing here.

There is a myth about the evolution of the American college presidency that runs more or less like this: "Back in the day," college and university presidents were figures of towering intellect who spent comparatively little time worrying about such mundane and vaguely unsavory things as fundraising and balancing budgets but instead provided visionary leadership for their institutions and, even more broadly, spoke with effect to the great issues of the day.

Now, like many myths, this one has embedded within it at least some small element of truth. There have been in fact a handful of college presidents who have functioned as visible public intellectuals, and as the business of running a college has become more complex, the need for presidents to attend to matters financial has grown accordingly. If the past year has taught us anything, it is that not only college presidents, but business people and politicians and individuals of every stripe should pay very careful attention to the advice offered to Dickens's David Copperfield by the irrepressible Mr. Micawber: "Annual income twenty pounds, annual expenditure nineteen and six, result happiness. Annual income twenty pounds, annual expenditure twenty pounds and six, result misery." It is a president's job to avoid institutional misery.

But anyone who believes that this responsibility is new, or that college presidents used to be free of such concerns, is deeply mistaken. Here is one president lamenting the financial pressures of the job: "What I was sent here for is an inscrutable mystery. I am too diffident to wrestle with men about money or with financial problems so vast…. If [a college president] can read and write, so much the better, but he *must* be able to raise money." The voice is that of James Wallace, Macalester's fifth president, writing in 1895.

The reality is that college presidents have *always* had to be concerned with what someone has termed both the business of education, or the work of preparing students to be successful in their personal, professional, and civic lives, and the education business, or the work of ensuring that the institution can pay its bills. Bill Bowen, the former president of Princeton University, recalls being told by a Nobel-prize winning physicist on his faculty that "excellence can't be bought…but it has to be paid for." Bowen, who went on to become president of the Mellon Foundation, never forgot this observation, nor should anyone whose responsibility it is to seek the highest quality in education at any level.

The question of the extent to which a college president should function as a public intellectual is more interesting and the answer, in my view, more nuanced. Few would argue with the assertion that within the college community the president should provide intellectual, ethical, and even temperamental leadership. The faculty is responsible for shaping the curriculum and carrying out the core educational work of the college; the president can aid that work by articulating, clearly and repeatedly, the context within which it takes place and the ends to which it is directed.

At Macalester I believe the central end to be the education of students for what the ninth president of the college, Charles Turck, termed "the duties of world citizenship," which I take to mean preparation for socially responsible leadership and constructive participation in local, national, and transnational communities. Our job is to provide students with the knowledge, skills, understanding, and motivation to lead more rewarding lives themselves and to make a difference in the lives of those around them. It is to repay families and donors and the broader society, all of whom have invested in your education, by turning you loose after four years as smart, motivated people who will make the world a better place—and along the way to prepare you for some sort of gainful employment.

Further, a college president should be expected to model those attributes that are to a learning community most essential, including clarity of language and thought, civility, scholarly curiosity and rigor, openness to views that are different from one's own, and an unwavering commitment to ethical behavior: in other words, everything that we have *not* seen manifested at the recent town hall meetings on health-care reform.

Being human, college presidents will sometimes fail to meet

these exalted standards, but every day and in every setting they should try. This is important because, fairly or not, members of the community will extrapolate from the actions of the president a sense of what is valued and accepted by the college. For instance, if the president attempts to demonstrate regularly that she or he is the smartest person in the room—a habit that most of us acquire quickly in graduate school—others will assume that this is the appropriate goal to chase in an educational setting, whereas for me a more appropriate goal is for each of us to behave as if we are the person in the room with the most to learn. It's amazing how much better that works if one's goal is actually to learn something.

Things get trickier when the question becomes the following: what role should a college president play in relation to the many political and social questions that extend far beyond the borders of the campus and in many cases divide our communities and our culture? This is, I confess, perhaps the single most difficult dilemma that I wrestle with in my position. As those who know me well will confirm, I am by nature a person with strong opinions and a preference for expressing them directly: after all, I grew up in New York City, which is not a place known for its delicacy and decorum. At my family's dinner table, if you weren't shouting, someone would ask if you were feeling okay. I am also enormously frustrated by the absence of thoughtful public discourse in this country and believe that those who are educated and who embrace rather than mock the life of the mind have a responsibility to raise the level of that discourse.

And yet—fairly or unfairly, reasonably or not—the views expressed by the president are typically seen as the views of the college that she or he represents. My personal desire to express publicly my opinions on controversial issues often comes into direct conflict with my professional responsibility to preserve academic freedom and an atmosphere of openness to all reasonable perspectives that are civilly stated. And in the end that professional responsibility must take precedence.

Again I turn to Bill Bowen, who wrote that "the university should be the home of the critic, welcoming and respectful of every point of view; it cannot serve this critically important function if it becomes the critic itself, coming down on one side or another of controversial issues.... It is the freedom of the *individual* to think and speak out that is of paramount importance, and safeguarding this freedom requires that the institution itself avoid becoming politicized." There is no truth about Macalester in which I believe more deeply and, simultaneously, to which it is more challenging for me to adhere.

But my conviction is that in agreeing to become a college president, a willingness to be measured and restrained in one's public statements—to accept one's status as a walking, talking logo—is part of the deal. There is no principle that has generated more debate on campus. Some of you in this room will no doubt engage me in that debate in the coming years, and that is on balance a good thing. It is to wrestle with such difficult matters that college communities exist, and it is through such discussion that we approach closer to some kind of wisdom.

Now, this does not mean that I believe that I should say nothing about anything, though I'm sure there are those who think I do a pretty darn good job of saying nothing about everything. It means that I believe that I need to pick my spots with great care. In general, when I speak to issues of public significance, I try to focus on those that I take to be so central to the educational mission of Macalester as to require the college to make a decision about its policies and practices. Admittedly the line here is very fuzzy, and what one person considers central to our educational mission, the next might consider irrelevant.

But life is composed of such ambiguities.

My point might be made more clearly through the use of a few examples. It seems to me inappropriate for me in my role as president to endorse a particular party or candidate in the race for the governor of Minnesota. I have opinions—boy, do I have opinions—but to express them very openly runs the risk of suggesting that Macalester is taking an official, institutional position and even of jeopardizing our status as a tax-exempt organization. Similarly I do not believe that I should be staking out through my public remarks Macalester's position on health care reform or cap and trade or military intervention in Afghanistan.

These are however precisely the issues that all of you should be studying, arguing about, and taking action on through your lives as students, scholars, and global citizens. My job is to ensure that Macalester provides the environment within which you can do these things, rather than to delineate in each instance the proper "Macalester" stance.

On the other hand, I have spoken out both individually and on behalf of Macalester on issues including the importance of diversity to higher education and the necessity for all of us to practice and model environmental responsibility. For me, these issues are inseparable from and directly relevant to our work as a college and therefore ones that I can and should address. So we have taken such public actions as signing an amicus brief in the University of Michigan affirmative action case and becoming early signers of the College and University Presidents' Climate Commitment. I would be prepared to contend that *not* to take stands on issues of this kind would actually impair our ability to carry out our educational work—and therefore that they are issues to which I should speak, both individually and as a representative of Macalester.

Again, is the line between issues of the first sort and issues of the second perfectly clear? Absolutely not. Is it important for anyone in my position to recognize that such a line exists and to decide on which side of it any particular issue falls? To that question my answer is yes. So those of you who will want Macalester during the coming years to take a position on a matter close to your heart should bear in mind that the standard I have described is the one that I consistently apply and should try to construct arguments that will meet that standard. And remember: it is *not enough* to argue that the majority of members of our community share a particular position on a cause or issue. One of my tasks—indeed, one of the tasks for all of us—is to create an environment within which the views of the minority can be freely expressed and listened to carefully, critically, and with respect. We do not achieve this by putting the weight of the college in every instance behind the views of the majority.

One of the most comfortable and at times energizing things about Macalester is that there is so much more consensus about potentially divisive matters than there is in the society at large. I suspect that this is why a fair number of you elected to enroll here. Bear in mind, however, that this is also one of the most challenging things about Macalester. It is a little too easy to get swept up in the collective certainty, a little too easy to dismiss those with whom one disagrees, a little too easy to become intellectually lazy. It is even, on rare but memorable occasions, too easy to become cruel. We never want to become mirror images of those whose intolerance we are constantly striving to rise above.

I wish I had foolproof advice about how to avoid these things. The best I can do, I guess, is draw for my wisdom upon that great example of popular culture and famous Twin Cities touchstone, *The Mary Tyler Moore Show*, which to most of you in this room is I suspect some sort of antediluvian artifact.

There is one episode of that show in which Ted Baxter, the buffoonish anchorman, asks Lou Grant, his gruff producer, how to be a better person. I believe this is just prior to Ted's marriage to Georgette, for those of you who are Mary Tyler Moorian scholars. Lou is initially at a loss for words, but then turns to Ted and says the following: "You know the way you are? *You know the way you are?* Well, don't be that way." So, if you find yourself casually dismissive of views that are different from your own—don't be that way.

I'm not sure in the end that I've provided an answer to those two students who asked me what I do—except, perhaps, to say that I try to do what all of us in a college community should try to do, and that is to learn from those around us and translate what we learn into wiser, more humane, and more constructive behavior. That's a hard job but one I wouldn't trade for any other. Best wishes to all of you for a wonderful year in this wonderful place. ∎

Ozzie, Harriet, and James B. Conant

A version of this essay was published in *The Chronicle of Higher Education,* February 22, 2013

Criticizing college and university presidents these days seems almost too easy—like poking fun at a Kardashian—and so, by current standards, Scott Sherman's recent piece in *The Nation* strikes me as relatively mild and balanced. In "University Presidents— Speak Out!" he takes college leaders to task for not following in the footsteps of such earlier, courageous leaders as James B. Conant of Harvard and Robert Hutchins of the University of Chicago, who took bold public stands on important and contentious issues. His position is pretty well summed up by his quotation from Andrew Hacker and Claudia Dreifus:

"Once upon a time, university leaders were seen as sculptors of society," but now they "are chiefly technocrats, agile climbers who reach the top without making too many enemies or mistakes."

"Once upon a time" is an apt way to begin the last sentence, since its version of history is largely a fairy tale.

I want to acknowledge, first, that I actually agree in large part with Sherman's central point. College and university presidents today are as a group less likely to speak to contentious issues than were their predecessors of the 1940s or 1950s, and their (our) collective ineffectiveness in making the case for higher education generally and liberal education in particular has allowed other voices to shape public discourse in decidedly unhelpful ways.

I would, however, offer some correctives to Sherman's argument, and certainly to the hyperbole of Hacker and Dreifus. While it is of course natural for a sitting college president to bristle at the claim that today's typical college president is a pusillanimous technocrat, bristle I must. Here are the important points that I think Sherman completely misses:

First, if the nature of the college presidency has changed over the past several decades—more fundraising and financial management—so too has the nature of the world in which the presidency is situated. For better or worse—and I think there is some of both—universities are not viewed today with the fairly automatic reverence with which they were viewed in the middle of the 20th century. To attribute this entirely or even chiefly to quiet presidents is to ignore a large set of much more powerful historical trends, including the general dumbing down of our public discourse and the anger provoked by rapidly escalating college costs. Does anyone seriously believe that if Drew Gilpin Faust, the President of Harvard, made a long public statement on the importance of gun control, it would change the nature or outcome of what passes for Congressional debate?

And then there is the Internet. James B. Conant had to wrestle with neither Facebook nor Twitter. He lived at a time when public debate proceeded at what might be termed now a stately pace, and when the worst someone was likely to do in response to an objectionable presidential statement was write an angry letter. Today there can be petitions, virtual protests, and thousands of fulminating blog posts within hours. The potential impact of a president's statements or actions on the institution of which she or he is the most visible representative has been magnified a thousand-fold, something that naturally inspires a greater degree of caution.

Second, there was no golden age. Individuals like Conant and Hutchins were always the exception—that is why they are so frequently cited—and there are exceptions today, several of whom are mentioned in Sherman's article. And let us remember that the institutions over which these moral giants were presiding were at the same time knowingly carrying out policies of anti-Semitism, racism, and sexism that their leaders did little to bring to light or change. Today's presidents are leading institutions that are far from perfect but are on the whole dramatically more open and fair in their practices. There is a curious Ozzie and Harriet-like quality to this yearning for the halcyon days of Ivy League universities in the 1940s.

Maybe most surprising, Sherman makes no mention at all of the critical importance of preserving the college or university as a place where opposing opinions on contentious issues can be openly and civilly expressed. A stand taken by the president on any such issue does not preclude such open expression, but it certainly has the potential to inhibit it, particularly among untenured faculty members or other employees who might disagree with the president and feel vulnerable. It is precisely because the president is what Sherman describes—the most influential public voice of the institution—that she or he must weigh the benefits of every statement on a controversial question against the potential stifling of campus debate. Different situations will lead presidents to different conclusions, but it would be a grave lapse in judgment to dismiss this challenge entirely.

I have always believed that courageous views, thoughtfully expressed, were actually less risky than silence in the face of serious wrong. I have spoken out, in my role as President of Macalester College, on many contentious issues, and I have chosen to remain silent on others. What has guided my decision-making, and what I believe guides the decision-making of most of my colleagues, is not cowardice or self-interest, but careful judgment about what is in the best interest of the institutions we hold in trust.

One final point: If Hacker and Dreifus are correct and college presidents are guided by the desire to avoid making enemies, we have mucked that job up as well. ■

The American College and Responsible Social Action

Portions of this essay were published in *The Chronicle of Higher Education*, March 18, 2013

The central function of colleges and universities is to educate, primarily their own students but also, and especially at research institutions, the broader society through the creation and dissemination of new knowledge. This may strike some as so obvious as to be virtually a tautology, though it is easy to forget while reading about the misplaced priorities of Division I sports programs or while listening to those who believe that education has no value beyond the purely vocational. Our higher education industry has become so diversified in its activities—the more critical might say unfocused or misguided—that its core work can be surprisingly simple to overlook.

Among the many forces threatening to pull colleges and universities away from that core work, none may be more powerful, persistent, and challenging than the pressure to take positions on a variety of social and political questions: that is, to go beyond education narrowly defined and act more directly as an agent of social change. Generally this pressure comes in its strongest form from students, who may in turn enlist support from alumni and faculty members. On occasion it will originate within the faculty, though I have found that faculty members typically expend their strongest energies on institutional rather than external political matters. The actions encouraged (or demanded) are most often financial in nature—divestments, boycotts, and the like—though sometimes they are more symbolic, as when a college issues a statement for or against a public policy or sends a letter urging an elected official to vote in a particular way on a particular piece of legislation.

My interest here is in trying to understand why colleges are so regularly subject to this pressure and under what conditions social action might or might not be consistent with the work of education.

I.

From time to time, of course, most organizations of any size will be asked to take positions on issues that sit at some remove from their core activities. In my own state of Minnesota, for instance, a divisive ballot initiative on same-sex marriage led to calls for many businesses to state clearly their position on the question, and a few did. In the wake of the horrific shootings in Newtown, Connecticut, many groups with no direct connection to firearms took visible stands on the issue of gun control.

But I would submit that no organizations are so regularly asked to take positions on issues to which they have only a tangential relationship as colleges and universities. While Macalester College is known for its high level of social and political engagement, it is by no means an outlier, and in just the past few months the "college"—by which the petitioners generally mean the administration—has been asked to take institutional positions on both the Minnesota marriage amendment and the Minnesota voter ID amendment; to boycott a particular hotel chain because of a labor dispute; to boycott a particular bank because of its foreclosure practices; to support the "Dream Act"; to sign on to an *amicus* brief to the United States Supreme Court in the case of Fisher v. University of Texas, which relates to affirmative action; and to divest our endowment of all holdings in fossil fuel companies because of their role in hastening climate change. This has not been an unusual year.

In speculating about why this is the case, it is tempting to say simply that college students are typically young adults who are on average more passionate about social change than older adults and who on average have more time and energy to devote to social and political causes. While generally true, this statement oversimplifies the situation and underestimates both the extent to which students are thoughtful and the extent to which colleges and universities are themselves responsible for the social activism within their communities.

In pushing for collective social or political action, students are arriving at a reasonable interpretation of things they are told by the institutions they attend. Especially at residential colleges, they are told upon arrival that they are joining a community with a shared set of values and standards; that the work of education extends beyond the classroom into the lives they lead in all settings; that the boundaries between the campus and other local and global communities are permeable and should be crossed; and, maybe most important, in the words of Macalester's rather typical "Statement of Purpose and Belief," that they have become part of a community that "models and promotes academic excellence and ethical behavior."

It takes no great leap of logic to conclude from all of the above that colleges should regularly take collective action to address issues in the broader community that have clear ethical dimensions. This is not to say that such a conclusion is in the end correct; it is merely to say that it is reasonable, and that attempts casually to dismiss such a conclusion as transparently wrong tend to oversimplify a complex question. I would cite as an example of such an oversimplification the well-known report issued by the "Kalven Committee" at the University of Chicago in November 1967 on "The University's Role in Political and Social Action." In that report, which is powerful and carefully crafted, the university is defined as a community "but only for the limited, albeit great, purposes of teaching and research." Were this in fact the message delivered consistently to students, one would be justified in using it as a basis for neutrality on all questions that do not pertain directly to teaching and research.

But when the same university in its current promotional prose also says that it is "enriched by and invested in the [Chicago] community we call home" and that it is "driven…to leverage our knowledge to enrich all human life," the definition and contours of *community* become less precise and the scope of appropriate institutional action more debatable.

Students at the University of Chicago might ask (and no doubt have asked) how the university can be "invested" in the local community if it remains silent on issues affecting that community and how it can be driven to "enrich" human life while taking no action to combat policies or organizations that have, in their view, the opposite effect.

Students at places like Chicago and Macalester are young but they are also bright and persistent; they notice and pounce upon such ambiguities and inconsistencies. The Kalven Report was prompted by the early stirrings of the widespread wave of student activism that arose on college campuses in response to the war in Vietnam and that was generally more unruly and disruptive than the activism seen today. It was also driven in my view by a very different relationship to the college as an institution. For the student activists of four decades ago, the college was suspect simply by virtue of being an embodiment of authority. The prevailing assumption was that authority was inherently co-opted and corrupt and needed therefore to be met as regularly as possible with resistance. (A popular Macalester pin from the 1970s, resurrected with pride at reunions, reads simply "Question Authority.") Thus colleges became the site of many anti-war protests despite the fact that most had almost no direct involvement with the prosecution of the war.

For most student activists today, the prevailing assumption is that the college has both the responsibility and the *capacity* to do good. Authority in most of its forms is less reflexively viewed with suspicion by the current generation of undergraduates, many of whom seek to be co-equals with rather than conquerors of those in positions of perceived power. Activism therefore is less often implacable resistance to authority itself and more often an expression of anger or disappointment that authority is not being exercised as responsibly as it might. The goals of such activism are more focused and its strategies more sophisticated and more carefully targeted. With some exceptions, these are serious and thoughtful efforts that merit a serious and thoughtful response.

II.

I would contend that there is no single, simple rule that applies easily and in all cases to questions of college or university engagement with social or political action. There are, however, some important lessons that I have learned during a decade of wrestling with these questions.

It is better and more accurate to frame decisions about taking institutional positions in terms of choices than in terms of absolutes. In deciding whether or not to take a position on a social or political issue, a college is never simply expressing approval or disapproval of a particular policy or practice. It is *making a choice* between competing priorities, one of which is always the profound importance of preserving the college as a place of free and open discourse, where opinions of all sorts on even the most controversial issues can be openly and civilly expressed. To the extent that the college takes a position on one of those controversial issues, it risks placing an informal constraint on the expression of opinions by in effect declaring that some are more just than others. Because the former priority is so important and so central to the college's reason for being, it should only be compromised under unusual circumstances and for a very clearly understood set of reasons.

Some forms of action entail additional choices: a boycott that might lead to increased purchasing costs or reduced investment returns, for instance, should be considered in relation to such potential consequences as budget cuts or tuition increases. Since the single thing at which colleges are least adept is stopping or curtailing any program or activity, such considerations can prove instructive.

This slope is very slippery. The collective memory of a college community is very long, if less than perfectly accurate. One can be sure that any decision to take an institutional position on a social or political issue will be cited repeatedly as a precedent and as a reason to take a stand on other issues more or less similar in kind. It is very important, therefore, to accompany any decision to take an institutional position with a clearly articulated set of reasons why the issue in question meets a criterion or set of criteria that most social and political issues do not. It is much better to do this at the time of the decision than after the fact, though it is also the case that such distinctions are much more likely to be forgotten than is the decision itself.

The world is full of people and organizations that do bad things. The decision by the college not to express an official view on, or take an action in response to, any one of these bad things does not constitute approval or complicity. And the mere fact of something being bad in the view of most reasonable people does not itself constitute a reason for the college to act.

It is very difficult to define the contours and determine the views of a college community. A "college" is comprised of multiple constituencies, each of which has its own priorities and each of which has a legitimate stake in the institution. These include students, faculty, staff, the Board of Trustees, alumni, donors, and parents. Within each of these constituencies, moreover, there are typically differences of opinion on virtually every issue of importance that relates to the college. No mechanism exists for determining a majority opinion, let alone a consensus opinion, on any meaningful issue among the members of these groups, so one should be very cautious in dealing with the assertions of those who purport to speak "for the college community." It is likely that this assertion has little foundation in evidence.

New forms of social media have made the currents of social activism considerably more challenging to navigate. To take only one example, Facebook has made it much easier for the few to appear to speak for the many and even more difficult to discern the point at which the "college community" ends and other communities begin. I have become convinced that one could create a Facebook page protesting an entirely fictitious act of institutional villainy and attract dozens if not hundreds of members, many of whom would have little or no discernible connection to the institution. The proliferation of on-line petitions and other virtual expressions of protest have, like the boy who cried wolf, made it much more difficult to distinguish genuine from manufactured outrage.

III.

Since the mid-1980s, when about 200 colleges and universities took actions of some sort to divest their endowments from investments in South Africa, calls to use such investment decisions as a form of social action at educational institutions have become common. Today the most visible and widespread effort is probably that of 350.org, a group founded by environmental activist Bill McKibben that is organizing students in an attempt to pressure colleges and universities to divest from all investment holdings in fossil fuel companies. This subject is important and complex enough to merit particular attention.

I would not rule out using investment decisions as a form of social or political activism in any and all circumstances, since certainly it is possible to imagine crimes so egregious as to deserve resistance and protest in all available arenas. But there is good reason to view the use of investment decisions for this purpose with skepticism and caution.

One of the commonly used arguments against divestment, particularly at institutions with large endowments, is that it would be extremely difficult. Such endowments are typically invested in diversified portfolios that include, among the equity portion, holdings in indexed funds, hedge funds, private equity groups, and venture capital funds. The stocks held by these various funds are numerous, constantly shifting, and even for investors often very hard to determine. Screening for particular companies or industries would mean not simply selling individual stocks but potentially changing altogether an investment strategy designed to provide, through diversification, both strong returns and limited volatility.

Another argument is that eliminating from an endowment portfolio an entire industry, particularly one that accounts for about 16.5 percent of the market capitalization of the New York Stock Exchange, runs the risk of lowering returns and increasing volatility, both of which could have damaging effects on the ability of an endowment-dependent institution to manage its finances and carry out its mission.

But sometimes difficult and risky things are worth doing, and the argument that divestment would be hard and might mean not doing other things strikes me as important but ultimately insufficient. While divestment advocates are rarely anxious to talk about those things they would sacrifice should divestment prove costly—programs? financial aid?—that might well be a discussion worth having, since at the very least one should be prepared for such a possibility. Ultimately my caution about the appropriateness of divestment is rooted more deeply in other concerns.

One needs to pay attention to whether any particular form of social protest is likely to be efficacious or symbolic or both. In virtually all cases, divestment is likely to be wholly a symbolic act, which is not to say that it is meaningless but is to say that it is unlikely at least in the near term to affect actual behavior or to be as powerful a tool as many of its supporters appear to believe. The fossil fuel divestment effort is a good case in point.

In round numbers, the current market capitalization of the top 100 coal, oil, and gas companies is about $7.5 trillion. The total value of all college and university endowments is about $400 billion, the vast majority of which is held by a very small percentage of institutions (Harvard, Yale, Princeton, and Stanford alone account for nearly 20 percent of the total). If one assumes that about half of that $400 billion is held in the form of equities (probably on the high side), that reduces the total to $200 billion. Fossil fuel companies, as noted earlier, account for about 16.5 percent of the market capitalization on the New York Stock Exchange, so if college investments are similarly distributed, that brings the total invested in fossil fuel companies to about $33 billion—or less than half of 1 percent of their market capitalization. This much might be gained or lost in a single day of trading. One would assume moreover that the equities sold by colleges and universities would be purchased by someone else, so the actual impact of divestment on the value of these companies would probably be nothing at all.

Still, symbolic acts can be powerful and important, so the argument about efficacy is not in itself disqualifying. More interesting, at least to me, are ethical questions that arise from the manner in which endowments are created and the purposes for which they are intended to be used. Typically college endowments are the product of gifts that have been given to the institution and then invested over time for the purpose of supporting the educational mission. Some of those gifts are restricted to certain uses—endowing a scholarship or a professorship, for example—and some are given to be used at the discretion of the institution.

While it is true that, once given, the gift is irrevocable, it seems reasonable to ask whether it is acting in good faith to take funds that were donated for the purpose, say, of supporting a scholarship for a first-generation student from Minnesota and use those funds to express disapproval of a particular company or industry. While most donors understand that investment decisions will be made by the institution to which the gift was given, most also assume, I believe, that those decisions will have as their goal maximizing returns while limiting risk so that the gift can have the beneficial effect for which it was intended. Is jeopardizing that goal for the purpose of social activism appropriate? While the answer to that question is debatable, I rarely see the question addressed by the more emphatic advocates for divestment.

I am inclined to see the possession of a college endowment not chiefly as an act of ownership but as an act of trust: trust with past donors and trust with current and future generations of students. This leads me to be deeply hesitant to stray, for the purpose of social protest, from the explicit purposes for which the endowment has been created and for which it is expended.

IV.

If one cannot arrive at a simple, easily formulated rule that determines when colleges should and should not take positions on various issues, one can at least rely on what I take to be reasonable and principled common sense, here expressed with characteristic clarity by William Bowen:

> ...neither individuals nor educational institutions should be compelled to take a position on every issue that others regard as highly consequential. To abstain is both a legitimate and appropriate action for a college or university when the issue is not central to the institution's educational mission. Universities need to retain control over their own agendas and to decide for themselves when it is, and when it is not, appropriate to take a position: looked at in this way, debates over affirmative action and discrimination

*based on sexual orientation seem to me entirely different
from debates over labor practices in the textile industry.*

Bowen's central points are worth underscoring: abstention is
not complicity; institutions need to control their own decision-making processes and not allow those processes to be dic-
tated by others outside the institution; there are times when action may be deemed inappropriate and, much less often, times
when it may be deemed appropriate; and the relationship of any
issue to the institution's central mission—education—must be
the critical factor in determining the appropriateness of action.
Note that none of this suggests that any particular decision is
easy or that there is no room for the exercise of judgment; rather, it suggests that judgment should be guided by a clearly understood set of principles.

Institutional activism poses two principal challenges to
the educational mission of the college. The first of these has
been exhaustively explored: to paraphrase Bowen, the Kalven
Committee, and countless others, to the extent that the college
or university *becomes* the social critic it jeopardizes its role as
creator and home of the social critic. Each time it declares that
there is a right answer to disputed questions, it runs the risk of
limiting the freedom of debate and inquiry. This danger is real,
though I must confess that in practice I have rarely seen the
declaration of an institutional position lead to a curtailment of
debate: if anything, given the nature of most academic communities, such declarations spark and intensify debate and so may
not be as dangerous as some fear.

I believe the principle of academic freedom, not to mention the spirit of disputatiousness, to be so firmly engrained
in our academic institutions as to be remarkably resistant
to limitation. Anyone who believes that the statement of
an "official" viewpoint leads faculty and students natural-

ly to fall in line has not spent much time on an American college campus.

More troubling to me is the potential for certain forms of institutional activism to make personal activism less meaningful, too *easy*, by shifting responsibility from the individual to a centralized authority and thus to undermine the educational goal, in the words of Macalester's "Statement of Purpose and Belief," of preparing students "to take responsibility for their personal, social and intellectual choices." This is especially true of such institutional actions as boycotts and the banning of a product on campus.

Several years ago I was importuned by a group of students to ban Coca-Cola products from campus because of the company's alleged complicity in the murder of union organizers in Colombia, a deeply serious charge but one that has never been substantiated by an independent investigation. Leaving aside the validity of the accusations, as well as the question of whether a shift from Coke to Pepsi represents an act of social responsibility, such a ban struck me as an unhelpful substitution of institutional for individual decision-making. In cases such as this, it seems proper to leave to each member of the community the choice of whether or not to patronize a particular company or purchase a particular product.

Similarly, when a group of faculty asked that I cancel a day of classes as an act of protest against the war in Iraq, my response was that acts of protest against injustice cannot and should not be *mandated* by provosts or college presidents or academic institutions. Indeed, such a mandate robs the individual decision to engage in protest of all force and meaning. No longer is it a personal choice or an expression of one's own belief; instead, it is obedience—neither freely chosen nor born necessarily of deep conviction to the dictates of an external authority. Freedom of choice—freedom of thought—means the freedom to act out of conscience in full awareness of the consequences of that action. It does not mean asking others to relieve one of both the burden and the gift of self-determination. It does not mean depriving others of the right to choose with equal freedom.

V.

Much as I wish that there was an easy way to distinguish between those issues that are and are not relevant to the educational mission of a college, I do not in the end believe that an easy way exists. I am more inclined to think about issues as sitting along a continuum, with those at one extreme of clear and obvious relevance—here I would include issues such as affirmative action and the importance of the Pell Grant program—and those at the other extreme forming a much larger group of matters that very clearly do not bear upon that mission. But it is only fair to acknowledge that there are issues that sit between those extremes and that will require institutions, as Bowen puts it, to "decide for themselves." No single, simple rule can in these cases substitute for the thoughtful exercise of institutional judgment or fully satisfy those who believe that judgment to be wrong.

While most who write about this subject understandably focus on the dangers created by colleges and universities saying too much on social and political matters, one should not ignore the negative consequences of their saying too *little* on issues that do affect their ability to carry out their mission. I believe that we have seen some of those negative effects in recent years as colleges, constrained either by a narrow definition of their mission or by sheer timidity, have remained far too silent on issues such as the importance to a democratic society of having an educated population, the dangers and fundamental unfairness of the educational achievement gap in our schools, and the true drivers of the economics of both public and private institutions. The consequence of this silence has been that others have shaped the nature and terms of the public debate and the reputation of American higher education has never been worse.

There is something reassuring about the notion that colleges and universities exist as organizations "only for the limited, albeit great, purposes of teaching and research." There is also something naïve and evasive about that notion. Like it or not, colleges and universities are social actors. As I said at the start, their chief social purpose is and always must be education, but this does not lead directly to the conclusion that they should in all instances be absent from debates taking place beyond the boundaries of their campuses.

The job of those who lead these institutions is to recognize that every decision to speak to an issue, and every decision to remain silent, will have meaning and will have the potential to affect in some way the ability of the college to carry out its mission. We must do our best to choose wisely both those moments when we will resist pressures to "take a position" and those moments when we will not be silent. ∎

On Governance
and Planning

The Great Ratings Debate

From *Macalester Today*, Fall 2007

Absent a personal scandal or similar disaster, small-college presidents rarely make big-time news. This summer, however, has been a bit different, as presidents representing institutions in the Annapolis Group—an informal organization whose members include about 125 of the leading liberal arts colleges in the United States—took up arms against the annual *U.S. News and World Report* rankings of American colleges and universities. While taking no formal action, the group indicated in a press release that, "the majority of the Annapolis Group presidents attending the annual meeting in Annapolis, Md., expressed their intent not to participate in the annual *U.S. News and World Report* ranking exercise." (I should note at this point that while Macalester is a member of the group, I was not able to be present at this year's annual meeting.)

The meaning of this statement is less than wholly clear, since to date only a minority of Annapolis Group colleges have taken a formal, public stance on the *U.S. News* rankings and since, in this instance, the impact of a decision "not to participate" is difficult to gauge. Most of the data used to construct the rankings in *U.S. News* are publicly available, so the magazine can get some more or less quantifiable information if it wants it. Reed College in Oregon has for years "refused" to participate in the *U.S. News* exercise, yet they are ranked along with the rest of us.

Probably what most rebellious presidents meant is that they will no longer participate in the reputational survey that determines about 25 percent of each school's score in *U.S. News.* In this survey—sent to the president, chief academic officer, and chief admissions officer of participating institutions—we are asked to rate the academic quality of a long list of "peer" schools. It is a silly exercise—what in the world do I know about the actual quality of what goes on at the vast majority of other colleges?—yet it plays a critical role in the rankings. It also pretty much guarantees that the rankings will turn out as the public expects them to and that there will be relatively little change from year to year: the best-known colleges with the strongest national reputations will naturally do best on a reputational survey. It is of course in the interest of *U.S. News* that this be the case: how much credibility would the rankings retain if Princeton, Harvard, Williams, and Amherst suddenly slipped to the middle of the pack?

As I ponder the appropriate decision for Macalester with regard to *U.S. News* (and I am, even as I write, pondering regularly), I am caught between competing impulses. On the one hand, I truly do believe that the *U.S. News* rankings are unreliable and misleading: they are constructed out of a combination of highly suspect reputational perceptions, financial indicators, and inputs such as SAT scores and selectivity. They speak not at all to the actual quality of the education or to the actual value-added at any college. They have led too many college applicants to switch from the right question—which college is the best for me?—to the wrong one —which college is the most highly ranked? And they misleadingly apply a zero-sum-game model from for-profit businesses to the very different field of higher education: whereas it is probably true that if Toyota improves its product and reputation, Ford suffers, it is not equally true that improvements at Macalester need to come at the expense of, or indeed bear any real relation to, the quality of what goes on at Vassar or Grinnell or Hamilton. Yet the rankings suggest that if we "rise," one of those colleges has to "fall."

Pulling against these concerns is my recognition that *U.S. News* will continue to publish its college rankings issue so long as it continues to be among its best-selling and most profitable ventures, regardless of whether college presidents criticize and complain. Indeed, it is not unlikely that these complaints will actually increase the impact and popularity of the magazine, since controversy tends to spark rather than diminish interest (as those who have attempted to ban books have never quite learned). If college presidents refuse to fill out the reputational survey, one can bet that *U.S. News* will not concede defeat but begin instead to survey high school counselors or corporate CEOs or some other group whose knowledge is equally or perhaps even more anecdotal.

And, in the end, my inclination is to think that more information is better than less, and that it should be left to the consumer of information to determine which forms are most useful and reliable. Attempts to suppress even the most baseless and scurrilous publications have rarely succeeded. Rather, it is incumbent upon those of us who dislike the efforts and influence of *U.S. News* to come up with alternative sources of information for college applicants that will in the end prove to be more helpful and reliable. Bad practice is defeated not by broadsides and boycotts but by better practice.

Our goal should be not to suppress the flawed rankings of *U.S. News,* but to make them irrelevant. ∎

Reflections on Faculty Governance and Culture: The Hedgehog and the Fox

Distributed to the Macalester campus, February 2008

Isaiah Berlin's great essay on Tolstoy's theory of history takes its title, "The Hedgehog and the Fox," from an aphorism attributed to the Greek poet Archilochus: "The fox knows many things, but the hedgehog knows one big thing." Berlin locates many of our greatest writers and thinkers in one of these two categories, not to argue that either comes closer than the other to some fundamental truth, but to suggest that hedgehogs (among whom he includes Dostoevsky, Dante, and Proust) and foxes (among whom he includes Shakespeare, Goethe, and Joyce) base their apprehension of the world on two dramatically different sets of assumptions and beliefs: the former relating everything in creation to "a single central vision" and the latter pursuing "many ends, often unrelated and even contradictory."

After a quarter-century as a faculty member and administrator, I have come to hypothesize that the intellectual and political life of a college may be understood as an ongoing series of struggles and negotiations between these two ways of perceiving and comprehending our particular piece of the world. On the one hand there is the core mission and identity of the institution, the "one big thing" around which and in whose service all else is presumably arranged; on the other hand there is the seemingly limitless number of narrower areas of interest and expertise that comprise and define the daily life of the campus: areas that we associate with departments and programs, with students and staff, with alumni and parents, and with all their many divisions and sub-divisions, each of which—always with passion and often with incisive intelligence—lays claim to an understanding of the college's true identity and competes for its share of a finite pool of resources, time, and attention. From this whirl of perspectives we draw both our energy and our deepest sources of conflict.

I have arrived, too, at the realization that among the most important jobs of the college president is to stand at the center of these relentless crosscurrents and serve as a sort of institutional hedgehog. That is, in accepting the responsibility of the presidency one accepts the responsibility to understand, articulate, and defend to the best of one's ability the "one big thing" that lies at the heart of the college, recognizing that it will always be contested and that it is impossible for any president to grasp in their fullness all of the "many things" known and believed by the individuals and groups that comprise the college community. Absent a president willing to play this role, most colleges will surely survive—we are tenacious about surviving—but will fail to take full advantage of their opportunities to excel or to establish a clear institutional direction. They will, in short, behave in the way that colleges and universities characteristically behave.

We can do better at Macalester; indeed, I would argue that we *must* do better if we are to sustain, let alone enhance, the levels of excellence achieved at the college over the past 20 years. Since the late 1980s Macalester has scripted one of the most compelling narratives in American higher education, in part through the good fortune represented by DeWitt Wallace and in part through the good decisions made by leaders within the Board of Trustees, the administration, and the faculty. Few would dispute the claim, however, that we are entering a period of change and challenges for private colleges, one marked by an unprecedented level of scrutiny of our economic models, our outcomes, our missions, and our efficiencies. The institutions that thrive will be those that do the best job of understanding and explaining their goals and of aligning those goals both with the public good and with their own activities and resources.

We are also entering a period, I predict, during which the gap in resources between a very small group of very wealthy institutions and everyone else will expand sharply. Absent the appearance of another DeWitt Wallace, and despite our best efforts to manage our endowment and strengthen our fundraising, Macalester will never again within any of our lifetimes be among the wealthiest liberal arts colleges in the country. On the contrary, the disparity in resources between Macalester and many of the colleges with which we wish to compete for students and faculty is much more likely to grow than to shrink, if only because a 10 percent return on an endowment of $2 billion is much larger than a 10 percent return on an endowment of $700 million, and because our comprehensive fee will probably remain lower and our discount rate higher than those of the wealthiest institutions.

And the growing disparity in resources is leading to a growing disparity in practices. Already we are seeing colleges like Swarthmore, Pomona, Amherst, and others begin to institute financial aid policies and add programs that we simply cannot afford under any foreseeable set of circumstances. The same is true to an even greater extent of the most well-funded research universities, whose resources have become virtually limitless. I do not expect this series of developments to change.

What we *can* do, and what I would argue we must do, is identify a finite set of institutional strengths that are neither measurable in financial terms nor easily replicable at other colleges and use them to guide our strategic decisions and internal practices. The good news is that at Macalester, more demonstrably than at most other colleges, such strengths do exist. Chief among these I would identify a longstanding and distinctive commitment to preparing students for what my predecessor Charles Turck termed in 1945 "the duties of world citizenship," which I take to mean preparation for socially responsible leadership and constructive participation in local, national, and transnational communities. Related to this strength is our location in a diverse and energetic urban center rife with both the challenges and opportunities that characterize the modern city. For several years, and with something of the tenacity of a hedgehog, I have been making these same points, and I will continue to do so. These are assets of incalculable value that resonate powerfully with the wishes and needs of all of our important constituencies; not to take full advantage of them would be a mistake of the first order.

I want to be as clear about what I am *not* saying here as about what I am. Certainly I am not saying that global citizenship and urban engagement are all we are about. It is critical to our future that we offer a broad-based, first-rate liberal arts curriculum taught by outstanding teacher-scholars; it is critical that we attract a talented and diverse student body and offer programs that address their interests and needs; it is critical that we hold to the highest of standards in all that we do. But is there a college or university of quality in the United States that would not say more or less the same things, and is it enough for Macalester—is it in the best interests of Macalester—simply to replicate in our efforts and programs the work of those others? I would contend that it is not, and that we are confronted with the challenge and gifted with the opportunity to do more.

All this I state by way of preamble to what is probably my central and doubtless my most controversial point: that if we are to secure our future and take full advantage of our strengths, it is time that we take another, careful look at a number of our current practices and assumptions. It is time that we re-examine the systems and behavioral patterns we have brought into being, and it is time that we think seriously about the costs of contentiousness and self-division. More specifically, it is time for the faculty to do this. My power is in most instances limited to my ability to exhort, inspire, and encourage individuals to lift their eyes from parochial if deeply felt concerns toward a common and compelling institutional purpose. The power of our by-laws, our history, and our culture places in the hands of the faculty many of the decisions that will prove most consequential for the future of the college. For this reason, and in order to maximize the chances for success of the incoming provost, I would encourage the faculty to bear each of the following points in mind as it goes about its individual and collective work over the coming months.

Faculty governance.

Given the range of tasks we are called upon to complete, and given the central role played by the faculty in the life of the college, we simply cannot afford to operate under a faculty governance system that is anything less than highly effective. By this I mean a system that makes efficient use of scarce faculty time, that is clear in its procedures and goals, that engages with broader institutional interests, and that produces good outcomes. I do not mean a system that is without conflict or spirited debate, which seem to me an inescapable aspect of self-governance among 200 people who are very smart and trained to be critical. The question I invite the faculty to consider is whether our current system of governance is highly effective and, if it is not, whether the problems are remediable. In particular, I would encourage consideration of the very broad and disparate set of responsibilities imposed upon the Educational Policy and Governance Committee; the nature of the faculty allocations process; the role played by the president in the process of reappointment, tenure, and promotion reviews; the limited latitude granted to the provost to exercise judgment and authority; whether the faculty meeting as currently structured is the best forum for serious policy deliberations; and especially the broad question of whether the faculty is being called upon to do work that would best be done by members of the staff or administration.

I can imagine that my last point might be construed as a threat to the autonomy or authority of the faculty, but in fact my intention is exactly the opposite. Often a faculty that gets too enmeshed in administrative work actually has diminished impact on major institutional decisions, since its energies are directed toward bureaucratic details—and often toward intra-faculty conflicts—rather than toward larger matters of policy.

I believe that we might liberate the faculty to think more broadly and strategically if we relieved it of the need to focus on smaller matters such as study-away decisions and the allocation of faculty research grants. I believe that the faculty might play a larger role in consequential decisions about the college if it could act with more dispatch and more often articulate positions that reflect a broad consensus among its members.

Faculty evaluation and the role of scholarship.

I have participated in the cycle of reviews for tenure, reappointment, and promotion at Macalester five times and have been impressed in each instance by the care, humanity, and impartiality with which the Faculty Personnel Committee applies the criteria for evaluation detailed in the faculty handbook. It is the (rather thankless) job of that committee, however, to apply the criteria approved by the larger faculty and not to redefine those criteria; for the latter, a fuller and more challenging discussion within the faculty as a whole would be required, and I raise here the question of whether it is time for such a discussion.

Two points in particular seem to me to merit consideration. The first is whether our criteria for faculty evaluation have evolved appropriately as our expectations of faculty and the nature of faculty responsibilities have changed. Where in the evaluation process is there a place to consider the merits and quality of civic engagement work? How do we judge faculty who are experimenting with new technologies and pedagogies? Does it remain the case that we want untenured faculty to assume a very small portion of the responsibility for service at the college? My sense is that these and other questions have not been openly discussed for quite some time, in part because those discussions promise to be challenging.

Most challenging of all might be the second point that seems overdue for consideration: that is, the particular role that we expect scholarship to play in the lives, and eventually the evaluation, of faculty. Let me venture this guess: Many faculty members are reluctant to raise this topic out of fear of being considered insufficiently rigorous or productive as scholars. So I will raise it, and by asking the question in this form: Have the expectations for scholarly productivity at Macalester grown to the point where they are distorting the professional development of our untenured and some of our tenured faculty and are working against other interests—such as teaching, advising, and course development—that we recognize as critically important? Have we moved closer to a university model and further from a liberal arts college model of the teaching/scholarship/service balance than is healthy? I am prepared to listen carefully to the argument that the answer to these questions is "no," and I embrace without reservation the notion that teaching at the highest level must be informed by serious and ongoing scholarly work in one's field. But the question of whether we are currently overemphasizing traditional forms of scholarship, behind which lies an interesting and powerful institutional history, should not be one that we shy away from discussing, even if it touches upon—indeed, perhaps because it *does* touch upon—our most firmly held beliefs about academic excellence.

Curricular innovation.

During the past few years, and contrary to perceptions that higher education is resistant to change, the curriculum at Macalester has altered rapidly and dramatically—perhaps more dramatically than at any time since the move toward a less vocational curriculum in the early 1960s. Many of these changes —including but by no means limited to the growth in Environmental Studies; the addition of a major in Applied Mathematics; the addition of instruction in Chinese and Arabic; the creation of concentrations in Middle Eastern Studies and Human Rights and Humanitarianism and the ongoing work on concentrations in Global and Community Health and Global Citizenship; the creation or revision of courses that engage with the Lake Street corridor—make more credible our claim to offer a set of programs that takes full advantage of our mission and location. Virtually all have been the products of the interests and ideas of members of our faculty and not of administrative planning, though they have in many cases been aided by various forms of administrative support.

I suspect that the next intense curricular debate within the faculty will be over the question of whether we are doing too much too quickly and whether we have the capacity to sustain all these new programs, and all our existing programs, at an appropriately high level of quality. This is the right debate to have, and I would not be surprised if the answer to the last question is no. If so, I hope that the response will not be to halt all curricular innovation and experimentation, but to make careful choices on the basis of broadly accepted institutional priorities and perhaps to take a few risks, recognizing that not all of our curricular trials will in the end prove successful. We also cannot simply take for granted that older, more established disciplines have more automatic claims on institutional resources than do newer ones or even that an existing program is by its very nature more legitimate or more important to the future of the college than is one that might be imagined.

My own vision for the Macalester curriculum of the next generation is one in which strength in the traditional foundations in the liberal arts is joined with innovative developments in areas consonant with our mission and location. It would be a bold curriculum that would attract both faculty and students who aspire to be leaders in their fields and attract support from those with faith in the power of higher education to shape the world for the better. It would of necessity be a curriculum that did *not* include every program offered at every one of our peer institutions but *did* include some programs distinctive to this college. It would above all be a recognizable product of the Macalester faculty even were the name of the institution to be left off the catalog.

Assessment.

This is another area in which the college has progressed, thanks largely to the relentless efforts of a small group of individuals and to the pressures applied by accrediting agencies and other external bodies. We have, however, not yet become an institution within which the importance of assessment is broadly embraced by the faculty. By this I do not mean that we should aspire to measure our efforts or our outcomes in mechanical or simplistic ways: in the end, the results of our work can best be judged by the lives of our graduates and will therefore never be wholly reducible to charts or tables of data. Rather, I mean that until we define with some clarity the nature of our near-term goals and attempt to determine with some precision whether we are achieving those goals, we can never do more than *hope* that we are succeeding in our mission. Assessment done properly is not about reductive measurement; it is about the honest and powerful desire for self-knowledge and self-improvement.

So consider this a plea from someone whose own knowledge of and experience with assessment is relatively limited: I hope that when cooperation is solicited by colleagues on the Macalester Assessment Steering Committee, or by EPAG, or by a group charged with strengthening our evaluation of teaching, faculty members will respond with open minds and in good spirit. It should not be the case that those who teach and therefore assess the progress of students almost daily should be resistant to the idea of the faculty and the college assessing themselves as well.

Trust.

If there is a single lament that I hear most often from both faculty members and administrative colleagues at Macalester, it is that we appear to manifest in our public actions, if not in our private interactions, so little trust in one another. This seems true despite the fact that, in my experience, most individuals working at Macalester believe in the mission of the college and work hard and in good faith to carry out that mission as they understand it. It also seems more or less equally true of dealings within the faculty and of dealings between the faculty and the administration.

It would take the combined efforts of a historian, a psychologist, a sociologist, and a philosopher—maybe—to understand the roots of this behavior. It takes no expert to see it in action: in our election of colleagues to committees whose judgment we then question and motives we find suspect; in the peculiar reluctance of many to engage in frank and substantive debate at (or indeed even to attend) faculty meetings; in the disturbing infrequency with which untenured faculty speak freely and openly in public settings; in our quick assumption of the worst intentions behind ideas that have not yet even been fully developed. We see it in difficult processes and in the proliferation of conspiracy theories. We see it, most painfully, in our sense of ourselves.

It may be that behavior of this kind is endemic to colleges and universities, where individuals are bound together by a sometimes rather loose set of ties and where both faculty members and administrators—despite the fact that they not infrequently exchange roles—seem bred to distrust one another. (I confess that even after 25 years I fail fully to understand this dynamic, since, on a purely pragmatic level, I cannot imagine what might motivate administrators to act deliberately in ways that are harmful to the college or antithetical to its mission. Those of us who do such work are certainly as susceptible to errors in judgment as are any other human beings; whether we are particularly given to deviousness is another question altogether.) Nonetheless the result over time can be enervating to all but the heartiest of souls, leaving a landscape, to cite Yeats, within which "The best lack all conviction, while the worst/Are full of passionate intensity."

Commonplace or not, such behavior is unfortunate, and I am enough of an optimist not to concede that it is foreordained or unalterable. I believe that we owe it to our students, to the next provost, and most of all to ourselves to think and talk seriously about how we might strengthen the sense of collective trust on campus and about how such a strengthening might benefit the prospects of the college. I believe that we have the capacity to be a college known for its collegiality rather than its contentiousness.

We know from recent surveys that the overwhelming majority of our graduates are pleased with and grateful for the experiences provided by Macalester. It seems barely a stretch to imagine that we would collectively be equally pleased with and proud of our own efforts and the efforts of the colleagues with whom we work.

* * *

I hope that the reflections herein will be read as a frank and collegial attempt to initiate discussions that seem to me timely and important and not as an attempt to control the outcome of those discussions or to preempt the authority of the faculty. For this I have neither the inclination nor the requisite familiarity with all of the relevant issues. In my very first remarks to the faculty, in the fall of 2003, I made two promises: to be honest in my discourse both public and private and to act always in what I take to be the best interests of Macalester College. I hope you will understand this document as an attempt to adhere to both of those promises.

Recently a senior member of the faculty recalled for me his arrival at Macalester in the early part of the 1970s, during the worst part of a financial crisis that very nearly caused the college permanently to close its doors. His most powerful memory was not of deprivation but of the fact that his colleagues elected to take a substantial cut in salary rather than force the layoffs of a large number of newly hired faculty members. Never again, I hope, will we face so painful a choice; but certainly we can honor and perhaps we can recapture the sense of community and institutional loyalty that such a choice embodies.

Let me conclude with the reassurance that Macalester is academically strong and financially sound, at no immediate risk of either a disruption of mission or an abrupt worsening of fortune. But we face challenges that can best be overcome if we recognize and embrace our distinctive assets and if we ensure through our practices and our culture that we work together as effectively and cooperatively as possible: if each of us, as it were, plays at least from time to time the role of a hedgehog in support of the institution we inherit and share. I would be pleased to be part of any conversations that contribute to this end. ■

On Planning and Prudence

From *Macalester Today*, Winter 2011

"We shall pull through..." —James Wallace, 1898

More than two years into the ongoing, global economic downturn, the members of the Macalester community have many things about which to feel some mixture of gratitude and relief.

This has been an unpredictable period for admissions offices across the country, yet enrollment at the college is at its highest level since 1971. We have continued to welcome outstanding students, and by most measures our recent classes have been the most geographically, racially, and economically diverse in our history. Retention and graduation rates are without question our best on record and rank us among the very finest colleges and universities in the United States.

The finances of the college are extremely sound, and we have continued a longstanding pattern of managing to balance budgets every year. We have cut our controllable program costs prudently but not dramatically. We have asked our faculty and staff to make sacrifices, most clearly through a salary freeze in 2009-10, but, unlike many of our peers, we have not have been forced to lay off any personnel or eliminate any major academic or co-curricular programs. Our endowment is well off its 2008 high, but, measured against virtually any benchmark, its performance has been among the very best in the country.

It is probably fair to say, however, that in many respects our most challenging times lay ahead of us. No one has proven particularly adept at predicting the future, and conventional wisdom has a rather consistent tendency to be wrong. Yet the following scenario, if not inevitable, is certainly plausible enough for us to take very seriously in our institutional planning:

(1) Slow endowment growth: Given the formula we use to determine our spending draw from the endowment and the magnitude of the downturn in 2008 and 2009, we know already that the amount we have to spend from the endowment will probably be about the same three years from now as it is this year. We cannot know what future growth will look like, but most economists are predicting a protracted period of returns that are below historical averages. Revenue from the endowment accounts for about a third of the college's operating budget.

(2) Rising financial aid: During the past two years, the rate of growth in financial aid has been several times the rate of growth in our posted tuition. Macalester is one of only about 70 colleges nationally that meets the full

financial need of all admitted students, and the level of that need has risen sharply. The competition for those students whose families can afford to pay full tuition has also become increasingly intense; many are opting to attend less expensive public institutions or institutions that offer large "merit aid" packages.

(3) Smaller comprehensive fee increases: Macalester's comprehensive fee increases during the past two years have been the smallest on a percentage basis in many years, and given economic realities and various downward pressures on pricing, it is likely that fee increases in the future will continue to be in this lower range. Since income from tuition and fees accounts for more than 60 percent of our revenues, the combination of faster growth in aid and slower growth in price is likely to prove challenging.

The economic vicissitudes of the past several years have reminded us of some important truths that will be helpful as we navigate through these waters. First, an economic model in which expenses grow more rapidly than revenues is not sustainable. Second, careful planning *matters*. Perhaps the chief reason for Macalester's strength during this downturn is that we anticipated in advance its possibility (if not its depth) and structured our finances accordingly. We were prudent in our decision-making and that prudence has made the difference between a challenge and a crisis.

I believe that planning will serve us well once again as we move forward. This fall I established a task force comprised of staff and faculty whose charge was to consider possible responses to a protracted period of slow growth. This spring that work will expand to include a variety of committees and other groups on campus. The central goal of all this work is not to diminish Macalester; on the contrary, it is to figure out how we can be both a *better* college and a more *efficient* college. Given the quality of the people at Macalester, our record of careful planning, and the powerful collective desire to do what is in the best interests of the institution and the students we educate, I have absolutely no doubt about our ability to become stronger tomorrow than we are today, regardless of the difficulties we face. Such progress has been in many ways the central story of Macalester for most of its remarkable history. ∎

Macalester Tomorrow

From *Macalester Today*, Winter 2013

A mong many people, the phrase "strategic planning" inspires roughly the same level of enthusiasm as does the phrase "driver's license renewal." This is unsurprising. Too often strategic planning exercises are slow, overly complicated, and unfocused, and too often the results are cautious and vague, sacrificing clarity and boldness for broad palatability. Such exercises can consume an institution's most precious resource—time—and yield few meaningful results.

This need not be the case. Properly conceived, strategic planning is a chance for the members of an organization to sharpen their understanding of that organization's mission and to adopt the right strategies for carrying it forward. It is a chance to strengthen and excite a community by identifying and supporting the best ideas its members have to offer. It is a chance to address challenges before they become crises and to turn opportunities into advantages.

Here in my view are the *wrong* reasons for the Macalester community to embark on a new round of strategic planning: because we have not done so in a while; because we have recently completed a major capital campaign; because we are only a few years away from our next accreditation review. All of these things are true, and all of them are typically cited as bases for strategic planning, but if they are the chief drivers of our work the process is likely to be mechanical and the outcome unsatisfactory.

Here are the *right* reasons: because to thrive as a college we need to become better as a college; because we are in the midst of a period of dramatic challenges and changes to higher education and particularly to high-cost residential liberal arts colleges; because we must figure out a way to make difficult choices that are informed by a shared sense of mission and purpose; because it will benefit our society if Macalester and places like it are successful in educating young women and men at the highest level. These are the drivers that have the potential to make strategic planning meaningful and truly important.

Because Macalester is by virtually any measure a strong institution, our planning can move forward with a sense of confidence in the future of the college. It should also, however, move forward with a certain sense of urgency, given some clear signs that the world within which we will operate will be one that affords little room for error. This year, for the first time on record, the discount rate for the entire student body will exceed 50 percent. This suggests both a level of financial need and a level of price sensitivity among prospective students and their families that we have not previously seen. Almost daily stories appear in the popular and academic press about the growing problem of student debt, the growing influence of "massive open online courses" (MOOCs) developed by top-tier universities, and the broad defunding of higher education at the state level. Were our confidence to become complacency, we would be making in my judgment a serious mistake.

This spring we will begin a process of strategic planning at Macalester. Though the structure of that process has not yet been set, it seems only fair for me to articulate at the start what I expect to be its basic parameters. I expect it to proceed at a pace that is not rushed but expeditious. I expect it to allow for extensive community discussion and input, but also for a group of manageable size to discuss difficult issues extensively and in confidence. I expect it to result in a plan for moving forward that can be broadly embraced but that is focused on a finite set of critical issues and that includes tough choices.

Among the questions that such a process must consider and take seriously, it seems to me, are the following: What changes to our practices and priorities seem most likely to place Macalester on a sustainable economic path? How can and *should* technology alter the way we do our work? What set of curricular and co-curricular programs will best prepare students for personal, economic, and civic success? How should our mission as a globally focused institution and our location as an urban college affect the choices we make?

I would encourage all who care about the college to pay careful attention as this planning process unfolds and to engage with it when opportunities to do so present themselves. This is important.

We have volumes of information about what Macalester is today. The central question before us now is, at the same time, both basic and enormously complex: What at heart do we want Macalester to be tomorrow? ■

Other Musings

On the Public and the Personal

From *Macalester Today*, Fall 2003

The subject of my inaugural column for *Macalester Today*, and indeed my general approach to the column itself, was shaped by my lively conversation with an alumnus (Class of '59) at a recent gathering in Chicago. Commenting upon my interview in the previous edition of this magazine, and demonstrating the attention to detail and careful, critical thinking for which Macalester alumni are well known, he noted that the piece was attractive and clear in its message but that it provided relatively little sense of the "real" person underlying the presidential exterior. Of course he was largely correct. For all sorts of sensible and practical reasons, presidents, as public figures, spend much time articulating the ideas of most importance to the institutions they embody and not so much time revealing the subtler shades of their character. To do otherwise would be to neglect the job at hand and, perhaps, to invite scrutiny more probing and intimate than is comfortable.

Nonetheless, it strikes me that this column might provide some fairly regular opportunity for me to share with you some reflections less presidential than personal. All of you will have plenty of chances to read and listen to my observations on liberal education, civic engagement, and the need for alumni support—*especially* the need for alumni support—but, a few times each year, *Macalester Today* will provide a venue for my thoughts on issues more diverse and unpredictable, though I hope those thoughts will be at least of some interest and will connect, in one way or another, to our collective investment in the mission of Macalester College.

I've taken the ongoing title of my *Macalester Today* column, appropriately enough, from Charles Dickens, who edited from 1850 to 1859 a journal entitled *Household Words* that served in part as a forum for his views on the social, political, and cultural issues of the day. Among Dickens's many strengths was his ability to engage in a serious and sustained dialogue with his vast audience, and I will be pleased if I can borrow even a small portion of that gift as I speak to an audience considerably less vast but still united by a shared history and a shared stake in the present and future of Macalester. *Household Words* is meant to suggest as well my hope that I will be speaking in this column not merely from the office but from the home—not merely as the "president," but as the person.

So let me begin, this month, with a few revelations about the person. None of these is shocking or dramatic (sorry), but, to be honest, there's little that's shocking or dramatic in my present or past. Perhaps this is the first revelation.

It might be helpful to know that I am by nature a pretty competitive person, whether I am playing racquetball, which I do with indifferent skill, or presiding over a college of quality and distinction, which I hope to do with considerably more agility and force. At times I have regretted and attempted to rein in this competitive streak; at times I have acknowledged its contributions to whatever successes I may have had. Like so many defining weaknesses, this one may be inseparable from my defining strengths and may be, for better or worse, an indelible portion of my character. The good news for the Macalester community is that my desire to excel is inextricable now from my desire for the college to excel and will lead me to set for myself, and for the Macalester, the highest standards and aspirations.

I weigh today more or less what I weighed as a senior in high school. Some people find this obnoxious.

I find it difficult to take myself too seriously, a trait reinforced by the fact that my wife and children find it difficult to take me too seriously. As my younger son advised me shortly after our move to St. Paul, "Dad, on that side of the street you're the President. On this side of the street…" (a regretful shake of the head). This is, I believe, a good thing.

As those who have seen us around campus can attest, the Rosenbergs are a close family. Carol, Adam, and Sam are the most important parts of my life, and I am determined to keep them at the center of my life despite the demands imposed by a college presidency. This will be a challenge, perhaps the most daunting challenge of the position, but I am confident that Macalester is the sort of institution and community within which the challenge can be met.

I don't like mushrooms, olives, or raw onions. My wife, who likes to cook, finds this annoying.

Based on my assumption that readers can handle only so many startling revelations in one sitting, I will draw to a close with an anecdote and a final, serious, and utterly truthful confession. Recently I heard the distinguished American historian Edmund S. Morgan advise college graduates, with much frankness and not a little wit, that though intelligence, perseverance, and hard work were no doubt keys to success, the most essential thing of all was luck. "So go out," he said, "and get lucky."

I've been a very lucky guy. ■

"Charter'd Streets": Macalester and the City

From *Macalester Today*, Winter 2005

T he English Romantic poets, witness to the rapid urbanization of the British landscape, were among the first to write about the awesome energy and beauty, along with the ghastly squalor and cruelty, of the modern city. William Wordsworth stood on London's Westminster Bridge in September 1802 and marveled at

> *"A sight so touching in its majesty:*
> *This City now doth, like a garment, wear*
> *The beauty of the morning; silent, bare,*
> *Ships, towers, domes, theatres, and temples lie*
> *Open unto the fields, and to the sky;*
> *All bright and glittering in the smokeless air."* [1]

His contemporary William Blake gazed at the same city and saw something altogether different and less majestic:

> *"I wander thro' each charter'd street*
> *Near where the charter'd Thames does flow,*
> *And mark in every face I meet*
> *Marks of weakness, marks of woe."* [2]

One can only imagine what Wordsworth, Blake, and the rest of the boys would have made, two centuries later, of a world in which the city increasingly is becoming the *only* landscape many individuals ever see. As I noted in my last column, the urbanization of the planet is proceeding apace: presently about half the world's population lives in cities and within a quarter-century that proportion will increase to 90 percent within the United States and 60 percent worldwide.

Leaving aside the complex question of the extent to which this accelerating urbanization is to be celebrated or mourned, it seems clear that it cannot be *ignored* and therefore that the work of liberal arts education—the work of Macalester—must and should be affected by the changing demographics of the places from which our students will come and to which they will go. It is true that certain forms of intellectual and creative labor—the understanding of analytic geometry or the structure of carbon or the construction of iambic pentameter—may be seen as independent of time and place. It is also, true, however, that the work of being a scientist or teacher or artist will be deeply affected by, should in some sense be responsive to, life in an increasingly urban world. We at the college should think about this as we go about our business.

One of the most promising and distinctive features of Macalester is our location in the heart of a vibrant and evolving urban area. While no small number of colleges and universities are so situated, only a handful of these are residential liberal arts colleges of our particular kind and quality. Thus we are afforded opportunities unavailable to most of our peers to enrich the academic and co-curricular lives of our students. I speak not merely of the opportunity to sample the vanilla latte at nine different coffee shops, but of the opportunity to teach different things, or to teach things differently, because we are bordered by Snelling and Summit Avenues and not by rows of corn and alfalfa (against which, I should note, I bear no grudge). One of my more deeply held beliefs is that it is the responsibility of all faculty and staff at Macalester at least to *think* about the degree to which their work is or should be affected by our position in the Twin Cities, even if the quite sincere and legitimate answer in some cases is "very little."

The extent to which people are already both thinking about and taking advantage of our location is insufficiently known by many on and off campus. During this semester alone, Adrienne Christiansen in Political Science is teaching a course on women and politics that focuses on the Lake Street area in Minneapolis; Judith Howard and Beth Cleary in Theatre and Dance are partnering with the local Resource Center of the Americas and Patrick's Cabaret to create an installation and a performance; Peter Rachleff, Paul Solon, and Lynn Hudson are collaboratively teaching a history course on the global and local; David Itzkowitz and Peter Weisensel, also in history, are offering students the option of completing a public history project for their senior seminar; Michael Griffin in Humanities, Media, and Cultural Studies has students working on a documentary film on Lake Street; Julia Hess's anthropology class on globalization is also working with the Resource Center of the Americas. Given the space, I could compile a list several times this long with examples of other, exciting curricular and co-curricular efforts that draw upon, benefit from, and—in some cases—provide benefits to the city we inhabit.

And before anyone observes that the Twin Cities is not to be confused with New York or Boston or Los Angeles (certainly the case), let me add the following: we comprise the 15th largest metropolitan area in the United States and are home to the largest Hmong, Somali, and Liberian populations in the country and to one of the largest urban populations of Native Americans. Between 1990 and 2000, the percentage of the population comprised of people of color in the Twin Cities nearly doubled. Moreover, 15 companies listed in the Fortune 500 are headquartered in the Twin Cities, more than any city in America other than New York and Houston.[3] If we ever get to the point where we have exhausted the educational possibilities in our backyard—a point so far beyond the horizon as to be invisible—we can perhaps begin to ponder relocation to some alternative metropolis. Until then, there is plenty for us to learn, create, and support right here. ■

[1] "Composed Upon Westminster Bridge"
[2] "London"
[3] Information gathered from "Immigrants in the Twin Cities: A Snapshot," a report issued by the Greater Twin Cities United Way Research and Planning Department, August 2001; http://education.umn.edu/MN/diversity.html; and http://www.infoplease.com/ipa/A0108561.html.

The Role of Athletics and Recreation at Macalester

From *Macalester Today*, Spring 2005

People send me things: some nice—tokens of appreciation, bits of Macalester memorabilia—and some less gratifying, but either way the reception of such items is a necessary and expected part of the job. Among the "gifts" I received during my first year at the college was a copy of a cartoon from the November 3, 1978, edition of the *Minneapolis Tribune*. Beneath a drawing of a very young, very dejected football player walking beside what appears to be his father, is a caption—ungrammatical but to the point—that reads as follows: "If you're playing that rotten because you got some dumb idea you're going to go to Macalester some day, you can just forget it."

Presumably my anonymous correspondent wanted to remind me that the history of Macalester athletics has, at least over the past few decades, been less than consistently triumphant—as if I needed a reminder of any sort. From the moment of my arrival I have been invited to ponder the past and present struggles of our program in football and, more recently, in women's basketball, and to reflect even more broadly on the role of athletics and recreation on a campus such as our own. A few of those reflections I would like to share.

Most important to recognize is the fact that athletics form a central part of the lives of many of our students and that it is therefore incumbent upon all of us at Macalester to think seriously and constructively about the subject. About one in five students at Macalester participates in intercollegiate athletics, a far higher percentage than at nearly any Division I school, and many more participate in club and intramural sports. To virtually all of them, their shared experiences with teammates, coaches, and friends matter a great deal, regardless of scores and standings.

As for those scores and standings, it is helpful to remember that the results are considerably more varied than the conventional image of Macalester athletics might suggest. Not infrequently we lose; sometimes we win; occasionally we succeed on the highest level both collectively, as when our women's soccer team won the NCAA Division III national championship in 1998, and individually, as when Ben Van Thorre was named a first-team Division III All-American in basketball in 2004. Attention is paid, and rightly so, when our participation levels in some sports are unusually low, but attention should be paid as well to the very high participation levels in sports such as swimming and cross-country. And, clearly and consistently, our student–athletes are *student*–athletes: in 2003–04 our women's soccer team earned the highest cumulative grade point average of any team in the nation.

I am asked pretty often what success in athletics at Macalester would look like to me. My answer is simple: a program that comprises a meaningful, positive part of a student's educational and social life at the college, one upon which any alumnus can look back with pleasure and pride. From any academic or co-curricular program we should expect nothing less. This does *not* mean that we should yearn to win championships or measure success in simple terms; it means that we should do our best to provide student–athletes with the opportunity to succeed and to support them in their efforts. It means that any student at Macalester, regardless of athletic interest or ability, should find some opportunity at the college to participate in activities that promote health and fitness. It means we should work to integrate athletics and recreation into the intellectual and communal fabric of the college and not imagine them as a thing apart.

In this area, as in so many others, we need both to celebrate our successes and remain passionately determined to do more and better for our students. We need to think about recruiting and retention, and about budgetary support. We need to attend games and meets and provide congratulations and comfort. Perhaps most visibly, we need to create spaces for athletics, recreation, and wellness that are more inviting, useful, and flexible than those we have at present, the oldest of which were built during the presidencies of Warren Harding and Calvin Coolidge. Much more information will be forthcoming about the construction and fundraising plans for this project, but already I have been impressed by the passion, energy, and generosity of the alumni and parents who are volunteering their time and resources on behalf of Macalester students present and future. Without doubt, we will make this happen and we will do so soon.

Meanwhile, the cartoon remains tacked to my wall, a reminder. ■

What I Learned from YouTube

A version of this essay was published in *The Chronicle of Higher Education*, April 19, 2010

I am a middle-aged, balding college president who has no Facebook account. I do not blog. I have never "tweeted" and only learned to send text messages so that I might communicate at a distance with my children. The largest crowd I have ever addressed has been about 4,000 people at a Macalester commencement ceremony, and the number of people who actually read my regular column in our alumni magazine is I suspect relatively small.

And now, after agreeing to make a self-parodic video to be posted on YouTube, I have been viewed more than 25,000 times in a little over a week by people on every continent except Antarctica.* I have been linked to multiple websites and received several hundred emails from Macalester alumni—including a surprising number from the 1950s and '60s—parents, and students, as well as from other college presidents and from folks I simply cannot identify, and from countries including Pakistan, Japan, China, Spain, and Singapore. Not least important, we have seen the rate of gifts to our annual fund increase noticeably since the video was released.

I have, in short, begun to learn about the nature and power of the new forms of social media that are reshaping the way we communicate with one another and should be reshaping the way institutions and organizations of all kinds communicate with their constituencies. Traditional forms of communication have not lost their importance, but I suspect that without augmentation from these newer forms they will have a gradually diminishing impact. It is worth noting, too, that producing a video seen by tens of thousands of people within a matter of days costs a fraction of what it does to produce a typical issue of our alumni magazine.

A few lessons in particular are floating around in my head, though they have yet to assume a particularly coherent form. One is that the longstanding notion that colleges can carefully shape and control their public image is antiquated. Things that happen on our campuses, for good or for ill, assume a life and meaning of their own in the public sphere more rapidly and unpredictably than could have been imagined even a decade ago. Messages we send out, if they are not ignored, are reshaped and restated as in an elaborate game of "telephone." This does not mean that those initial messages are less important; to the contrary, we must devote to them more care than ever as we try to anticipate the ways in which they might be adapted and reinterpreted and the extent to which they might be appealing to forms of media that can almost instantly reach thousands or even millions of people.

Another is that we should never underestimate the power of humor and of positive messaging—particularly during periods of great social and economic stress. Like most college and university presidents, I have spent an enormous amount of time in recent months explaining and responding to the financial and political pressures that have been brought to bear upon higher education. This is my job, and it is important. Yet a recent study by researchers at the University of Pennsylvania reveals that people are most likely to forward on-line articles that are about *good* news. I would add (based upon absolutely no research) that I believe people respond more positively to individuals in positions of authority when they demonstrate convincingly that they do not take themselves or their responsibilities *too* seriously.

There are many things to bemoan about the current state of affairs in the worlds of both politics and broadcast journalism. I suspect that among the most frustrating to many people is the utter humorlessness with which individuals in both spheres proclaim their ownership of the truth and their self-importance.

Finally, and delightfully, I discovered that one of the observations I make often at Macalester is actually true. The creative arts are in fact a wonderful way to stretch oneself and communicate with others. They do help us bridge cultural and ideological divides. They are exciting and a great deal of fun. For these reasons and others they should play a central role in a contemporary liberal arts education.

I'm still not sure if people who watch the video are laughing with me or at me. But in the end, if they laugh, does it really matter? ∎

*Total views now exceed 82,000.

Remembering John B. Davis

From *Macalester Today*, Fall 2011

John B. Davis, Jr., the 13th President of Macalester College, died on July 5, 2011, at the age of 89. He would have been utterly uninterested in encomia but pleased to imagine that his passing might be used as an opportunity to ruminate on matters of interest and importance.

When I think of John—with whom I was privileged to become very well acquainted during the past eight years—I am inclined to reflect upon the subject of leadership. Macalester students, we have found, view leadership with more than a small dose of skepticism. Perhaps this is because we have as a society been "led" into so many dire situations; perhaps it is because there is no shortage of individuals more than happy to describe at great length the adeptness of their own leadership; perhaps it is because our students believe more deeply in the efficacy of collective than of individual action.

Historians, too, have in recent decades moved increasingly (though not uniformly) away from the notion that particular and powerful individuals are the primary shapers of historical events—the so-called "great man" theory of history—and toward a more nuanced sense that history tends to be shaped by social and political forces that are beyond the immediate knowledge and control of any single person.

None of this, I think, is fundamentally wrong. And yet—and yet—I hold fast to the belief that particular individuals of great character, courage, and ability can make an extraordinary difference in the lives of others: that there are in fact leaders who disproportionately matter in the evolution of communities and institutions. I believe this in part because of the example of John B. Davis.

While many people have played critical roles in the history of Macalester College, it seems to me fair to say that without the efforts of President Davis, Macalester would today be a different and in some regards lesser place and even that it might no longer exist.

When John assumed the presidency at Macalester in 1975, the college was fortunate in having a splendid faculty and passionate students but was confronted by some very serious problems, many stemming from the withdrawal of financial support by DeWitt Wallace and the consequent impact on the budget and operations of the institution. Like many financial crises, this one led not only to problems in balancing income and expenses, but to a fraying of the collective sense of confidence and of optimism about the future. One need only examine our national discourse during the current period of severe financial hardship to see how powerful and paralyzing this loss of confidence can become.

John understood that one of the great challenges of leadership, particularly during difficult times, was striking the right balance between candor and inspiration, between warning and inspiring people to rise to a higher level of excellence. His inaugural address, delivered in November 1975, is in many respects brutally honest—"we did not as a company of people deal directly and quickly with the economics of our college"—yet is never without a sense of confidence that "the great idea which is Macalester" would survive and thrive.

When John arrived at Macalester, the college faced a deficit of $2 million, very large in relation to the size of the overall budget. Within one year that imbalance was erased, and it has not reappeared in the many years since. Relationships with the college's largest donor, DeWitt Wallace, were repaired, setting the stage for the enormous gift that enlarged not only the college's endowment, but also its possibilities. Maybe most important, John established through his actions a model of trust, competence, and accountability that infused the entire Macalester community. At the time of his retirement from Macalester in 1984, one student commented that, "he will be missed not only for his work, but also for his character, which has allowed us to view him not only as a president, but in a way as a friend."

John would have been the first to insist that he was not solely responsible for the strengthening of Macalester during his tenure. In fact he did insist upon this, noting in 1984 that, "there have been some good changes since I've been here but I have been only one of the instrumentalities." True enough—though I would add that while John may not have been *sufficient*, on his own, to reshape the institution, he was indisputably *necessary*.

Anyone who knew John B. Davis, or who has read any of his writings, knows that he was fond of a Yoda-like inversion of syntax that never failed to catch one's attention. So in tribute to my friend and mentor, I will end thusly: most fortunate was Macalester to benefit from the efforts of this great and good man. A true leader he was. ■

A Column about Nothing

From *Macalester Today*, Spring 2012

"I think I can sum up the show for you with one word: nothing." —GEORGE COSTANZA

Writing a short column three or four times a year might not seem like difficult work, but let me tell you—after almost nine years the well begins to run a little dry.

How many times, and in how many different ways, after all, can I praise the values and virtues of a rigorous liberal arts education? (Some would opine that my capacity for repetition here is nearly infinite). Athletics? Done. The arts? Done. Alumni engagement? Done and done again. Global citizenship? To quote John McEnroe—you cannot be serious.

For the past several years I've been writing in one form or another about the *Step Forward* campaign for Macalester, but that campaign was concluded successfully at the end of 2011, and a call for everyone to *Pause* doesn't have quite the same inspirational effect.

So since nothing jumped immediately to mind as I pondered potential subjects for this column, I thought that I might try writing a column about nothing.

There is, it turns out, something of a literary sub-genre made up of works about nothing. A quick on-line search turned up more than a dozen poems ostensibly about "nothing," though in truth most of these are pretty awful and actually about the author's absence of any poetic gift. Here is my favorite quatrain, from "A Poem about Nothing" by an-author-who-shall-mercifully-remain-nameless:

The crashing waves of ecstasy
will me missing from my verse.
There will no expletive adjectives
or headless-chicken curse.

I have no idea what that last line means—so I suppose in that sense it is indeed about nothing.

There are several short stories about nothing whose quality is more or less in line with that of the poems and a hip hop/rap album called "Stories about Nothing." One of the songs on the album is entitled (and spelled) "Pergatory." Whimsical wordplay or misspelling? You make the call.

The greatest novelist to take a serious stab at writing about nothing might be Gustave Flaubert, who famously observed, in the midst of composing *Madame Bovary,* that "What seems beautiful to me, what I should like to write, is a book about nothing, a book dependent on nothing external, which would be held together by the strength of its style... a book which would have almost no subject, or at least in which the subject would be almost invisible, if such a thing is possible." Fortunately Flaubert failed in his attempt, since *Madame Bovary* is in fact about many things, nothing not being among them.

The visual arts also have their champions of nothing. Best known among them may be Andy Warhol, who noted the following about his Campbell's soup can series: "I wanted to paint nothing. I was looking for something that was the essence of nothing and the soup can was it." He may have come closer to realizing his ideal than did Flaubert, though it is worth noting that one of his soup can paintings was sold by Christie's for $9,042,500 in 2010. That's a lot of something for a painting of nothing.

But the artistic apotheosis of nothingness surely belongs to the composer John Cage, whose most controversial work, *4'33"*, consists of—you guessed it—four minutes and 33 seconds of total silence. I suppose one could also call the piece the nadir of nothingness, but since it consists of nothing that would be pretty much the same thing. It is the ultimate all-purpose composition, suitable not only for wedding and Bar Mitzvahs but for business meetings, political rallies, and professional sporting events. It is the only piece ever written that simply cannot be drowned out by crowd noise.

Anyway, I'm feeling pretty good about my own attempt to fill space with reflections on nothing. I've been checking the word count as I've been writing—not something I would recommend, since it's sort of like watching a clock hoping that time will pass more quickly—and somehow I have managed to make it to 679. 680. 681. That might not seem impressive if I were writing about something, but considering that I'm writing about nothing it—how fitting that the 700th word in a column about nothing is "it"—seems to me a pretty darn note-worthy accomplishment.

I will, however, accept no congratulations.

It was nothing. ■

Ten Years

From *Macalester Today*, Fall 2013

A fter ten years in my office, I decided recently that it was time to do a little bit of housecleaning.

The drawers and cabinets yielded some mildly interesting pieces of accumulated flotsam: something called a "musical can kilt," for those occasions when one wants to hear "Scotland the Brave" while downing a cold one; a Charles Dickens action figure, probably in anticipation of *The Avengers II*; and two Karl Egge bobbleheads, because, really, one Karl Egge is far from enough. I discovered too that I could wear a different Macalester-themed item of clothing every day for the rest of my life and never have to go near a washing machine.

I have the paint bucket trophy claimed annually by the winner of the Macalester-Hamline football game, a tartan deerstalker cap given to me by John B. Davis, and a *vuvuzela*, or plastic horn, presented to me by our Afrika! student organization and which I am forbidden, both at home and at work, to play.

My years at Macalester are exhaustively documented in photographs: in a nightcap, a headband, and a football jersey; with Kofi Annan, Paul Farmer, Chris Kluwe, and a cow; smiling, eating, and staring into the distance as if contemplating the mysteries of the cosmos. Truly, I have done it all.

More interesting than any physical memorabilia I encountered were the virtual treasures in my email inbox. Searching for the word *appalled*, I found 54 items; *outraged* yielded 137; *furious* turned up 186. I confess that I did not check to see how many times these words appeared in the same message, so my count might include some repeats. Surprisingly, *fulminating* appeared only twice. Four syllables are a lot to spit out when one is apoplectic.

I had forgotten—or chosen to erase from my memory—the pithy message that skipped all niceties and simply began with the forceful greeting, "You politically correct #%!!*#&%!" This particular gentleman, so far as I can tell, had had no previous relationship with Macalester, though I seem to have given him a reason to establish one.

I don't mean to make light of anyone's fury—well, maybe I do—but the truth is that after a decade in a college presidency one becomes surprisingly inured to these sorts of fusillades. Presidents get both credit and blame for many things with which they had little to do, and the key to maintaining both one's sanity and one's humility is to remain relatively unaffected by both the praise and the criticism: to separate the "president" from the person and to focus not on the response to what one did yesterday but on the opportunities to do better today and the day after that. That has always been and will always be the way I approach my work at Macalester.

It is also important to recognize what an enormous privilege it is to be part of an institution with the history and mission of a great liberal arts college. For nearly a century and a half, skilled and dedicated people have educated students from around the country and around the world to become successful and to make a positive difference in the lives of others. Generous donors and volunteers have supported that work with gifts of resources and time. We live in an age when cynicism and even despair come too easily, but to fail to be inspired by this is to fail to appreciate the best of which human beings are capable.

Three items in particular, all visible as I sit at my desk in Weyerhaeuser Hall, speak to me powerfully of my good fortune. One is a photo of the members of my senior staff. Granted, in this particular image their heads are photoshopped onto the bodies of the bridge crew of the Starship Enterprise, but still, there they are, reminding me of how much I have benefited from the talents of those with whom I work.

The second is a black-and-white photograph, probably taken around 1940, of Charles Turck at work at his desk in Old Main. He is smiling, and pressed to his ear is the handset of a black rotary telephone. Absent President Turck's principled and visionary leadership for nearly two decades, Macalester would be a different and lesser place and my job much less rewarding.

And the third is a handwritten letter from Vice President Walter and Joan Adams Mondale, thanking me for my service to the college. With apologies to our archivist, that one is coming with me when I leave.

To the Mondales, and to my colleagues, and to all in the community at whose pleasure I serve Macalester College: thanks for the chance. ∎

What I Learned

From *Macalester Today*, Spring 2014

Asabbatical is intended as a time for restoration and for reflection. Ideally, one should return from this interregnum with a new and richer understanding of oneself and one's relation to the world. A suntan is a nice addition but less essential.

For me, this period of sustained tranquility has been unprecedented. My only other sabbatical occurred 22 years ago, when my wife Carol was working six or seven days each week and my older son Adam was a year old: the list of things on the agenda at that time did not include much solitude and self-scrutiny. I wrote much of a book on Dickens, changed many diapers, and pretty much never left Erie, Pennsylvania, which would not have been my first choice of a place to spend free time.

I am of course keenly aware that most people in most professions go their entire working lives without having the opportunity for anything like a sabbatical (helpfully reminded, from time to time, by my spouse). I feel most fortunate to have had this gift of freedom. I wish our society embraced the understanding that we would collectively be more healthy and productive if more people had a similar gift. Many Europeans, for instance, seem to have incorporated a sabbatical into their working lives. They call it "August." And yes, they do seem to undermine the notion that sabbaticals and productivity are directly correlated, but I am convinced nonetheless that there can be a happy middle ground between the American (particularly male American) pride in working to the point of exhaustion and the Italian custom of the three-hour lunch.

Here are some things I learned during the past few months.

My friend Judith Shapiro, retired president of Barnard College, has said that since you're going to spend the rest of your life inside your own head, you'd better make sure that it's an interesting place to be. I learned that my head, gray and balding as it is, is not uninteresting, at least to its owner. I spent surprisingly little time from the start of September through mid-December thinking about Macalester, I paid almost no attention to the news, and I was just fine. Better than fine, actually: I was relaxed, curious about the things around me, and more focused than ever before on the present rather than the past or future.

I learned that one of life's hidden pleasures is driving long distances through beautiful and relatively isolated places with no need to be anywhere for a scheduled meeting or appointment. It helps if one is driving a car that can go really fast when no one is looking, but any reasonably reliable vehicle will do. California is by far the most populous state in the nation, but it is also very big, and I managed at times to drive 20 or 30 miles through heavily wooded hills without passing another vehicle. I explored almost every possible route back and forth between the town of Sonoma and the Pacific coast, and I drove long stretches of that coast on roads that seemed designed by an imaginative child playing with Lego. I listened to all my favorite music from college. I stopped for coffee in the town of Bodega Bay, where Alfred Hitchcock filmed *The Birds* and where, this being America, there is a "Birds Café" and a life-sized replica of Hitchcock outside a grocery store. I found a bakery and a cheese shop in the town of Freestone, pop. 50, that rival anything in New York. (Another highlight of Freestone is the famous Osmosis Spa, specializing in the Cedar Enzyme Bath. I did not indulge.)

As an aside, I learned that one of life's pleasures is *not* driving in Italy. As my friend and guide Guido Fratini says of his homeland, "One country, one highway." Every other road is narrow, winding, and pretty much unnamed. Throw in a traffic circle every 50 meters or so, the inability to connect with GPS, hundreds of crazed motorcyclists outfitted like Arnold Schwarzenegger in *Terminator 2*, and the occasional *cinghiale* (wild boar) wandering across the pavement and you have a recipe for mayhem. But the views: magnificent.

I learned to admire the craftspeople of the world, particularly those who fashion with dedication, passion, and honesty the things we eat and drink. I had a chance to listen to women and men who make cheese and chocolate and wine—how's that for a nutritional pyramid?—and was struck by the almost spiritual seriousness with which the best of them approach their labor. Those of us who work chiefly at desks and on computers tend to underestimate both the difficulty and the powerful beauty of transforming a giant pod into a piece of chocolate that improves a bad day or grapes into a wine that lingers for years in one's memory. The people who do this at the highest level are very gifted, and very smart.

The winemakers, unsurprisingly, captured my imagination with special force. There's Michele Satta, making brilliant wines in Bolgheri, who likens his role to that of an orchestral conductor. "Same music, same musicians, different conductors, different sound. Same grapes, same land, different makers, different taste." Hard to argue. Steve Law, from Edinburgh, was working as an electronics engineer for Hewlett Packard in Scotland and France before quitting his job to make cool-climate, French-style Syrah in Sonoma. (I tried to convince him to change the name of his wine, Maclaren, to Macalester, but learned that clan members, unlike baseball players, cannot become free agents.) Doug and Lee Nalle have been making Zinfandel, some from pre-Prohibition vines, in the same refined style for 30 years, regardless of changing markets or fashions. If not for the fact that I don't like to get dirty, hate bugs, am impatient, and prefer to live within walking distance of a place that makes a good *latte*, I could see myself doing this stuff.

One of the skills I have honed during my decade as a college president is what might be called "shmoozeability": the capacity to be at ease when conversing with new acquaintances and to ask questions that encourage them to be forthcoming about their interests. I learned that this skill is transferable to other settings and makes traveling considerably more enjoyable and instructive. My father was a master at this, and his endless string of conversations with total strangers used to render my siblings and me paralyzed with embarrassment. Now I know what he was up to and why he returned from every vacation with new friends.

I learned that the physical effects of stress are enormous. I knew this on an intellectual level, of course, but there is no sub-stitute for learning through experience. Put another way, the removal of stress makes one feel a whole lot better. Evidently some people can achieve this low-stress state through strategies such as meditation, yoga, and the philosophy known in techni-cal terms as "not giving a shit." I seem to lack this ability and to require the removal of the actual cause of stress in order to feel relaxed. Oh, well.

I learned, or was helpfully reminded, of the truth that there remains a BR separate and distinct from PBR. It is not the case that my presidential persona is in any important way inauthen-tic; like Popeye the Sailor, I am what I am. Rather, the picture of me as President of Macalester is only a partial representation: not photo-shopped, but cropped. After a decade of inhabiting an all-consuming role, one does begin to wonder if all parts of one's personality apart from the role have been consumed. I have been reassured that this is not the case. For better or worse, and with all its flaws, the part of me that is *me* is still in there.

And finally, and most important, I learned that the most complex, nuanced, and interesting California Pinot Noirs come from coastal vineyards, though they require the maturity that comes with age to reach their full potential.

This is a lesson we should all remember. ∎